Next of Kin

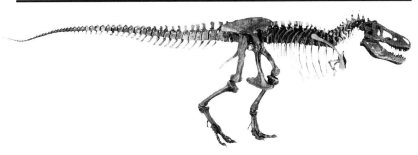

GREAT FOSSILS AT THE AMERICAN

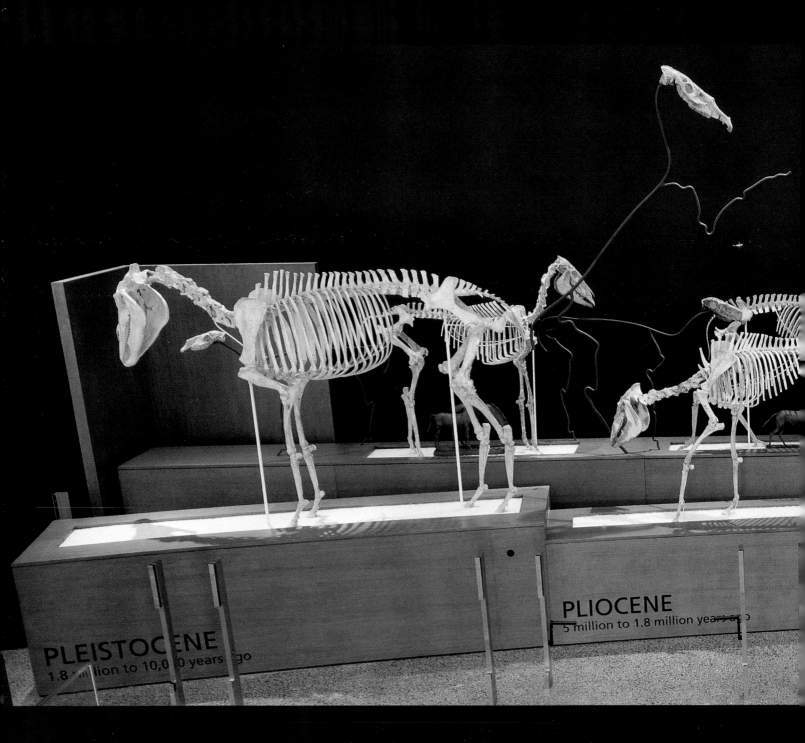

PLIOCENE
5 million to 1.8 million years ago

PLEISTOCENE
1.8 million to 10,000 years ago

MUSEUM OF NATURAL HISTORY
Next of Kin

LOWELL DINGUS

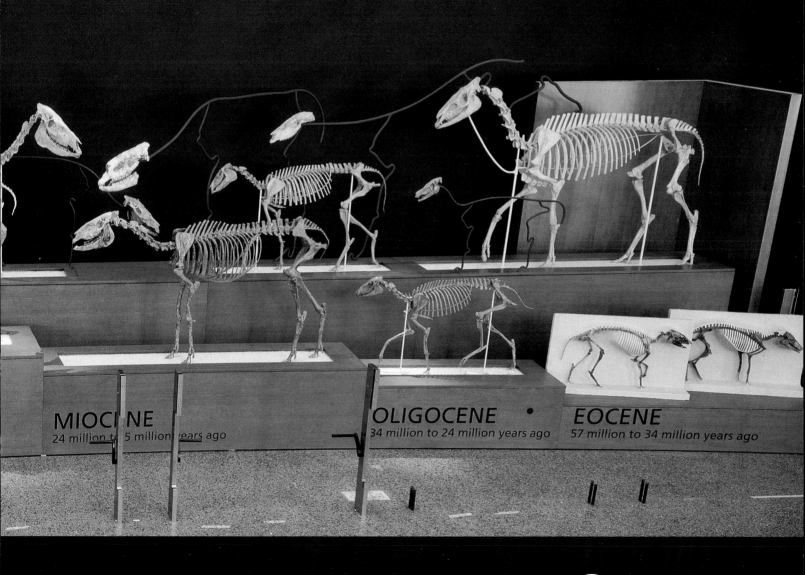

MIOCENE
24 million to 5 million years ago

OLIGOCENE • EOCENE
34 million to 24 million years ago   57 million to 34 million years ago

RIZZOLI
NEW YORK

First published in the United States
of America in 1996 by

RIZZOLI INTERNATIONAL PUBLICATIONS, INC.
300 Park Avenue South
New York NY 10010

Library of Congress Cataloging-in-Publication Data

Dingus, Lowell.
    Next of kin : great fossils at the American Museum of Natural
    History / Lowell Dingus.
            p.   cm.
    Includes index.
    ISBN 0–8478–1929–9 (HC)   ISBN 0-8478-1992-2 (PB)
    1. Dinosaurs—Catalogs and collections—New York (State)—New
    York.   2. American Museum of Natural History—Exhibitions.
    I. Title.
    QE862.D5D4927   1996   96–48881
    560'.74'7471—dc20   CIP

0 33666874

Jacket illustration and half-title page: Allosaurus *mount in*
The Hall of Saurischian Dinosaurs.
Frontispiece: Display of the evolution of horses in the Paul
and Irma Milstein Hall of Advanced Mammals, Lila Acheson
Wallace Wing of Mammals and Their Extinct Relatives

Designed by Abigail Sturges

Printed and bound in Singapore

CONTENTS

ACKNOWLEDGMENTS

The author would like to express his sincere appreciation to everyone who participated in the renovation of the fossil halls. More specifically, the constant support of the American Museum of Natural History's Board of Trustees is gratefully acknowledged, including that of Chairman Anne Sidamon-Eristoff, Chairman William T. Golden, Fourth Floor/Library Committee Chairman Daniel Brodsky, and Fourth Floor/Library Committee Chairman Frank Y. Larkin. The knowledgeable guidance of the Museum's Administration was also greatly appreciated, including that of President Ellen V. Futter and President George D. Langdon. Especially helpful was the consistent support and camaraderie of Provost Michael J. Novacek, Senior Vice President for Operations and Intergovernmental Relations Barbara D. Gunn, and Vice President for Communications Jeanne Collins. In addition, I want to express my thanks to the Museum's Department of Development for helping to generate the funding. Throughout the development and most of the production of this project, I benefited daily from the wisdom, empathy, and friendship of Director William J. Moynihan. To Bill, I owe an especially deep debt of gratitude.

The remarkable evolutionary story in these halls stems primarily from the exacting knowledge provided by the Curators of the Department of Vertebrate Paleontology, including Richard H. Tedford, Eugene S. Gaffney, Mark A. Norell, John G. Maisey, Michael J. Novacek, and Malcolm C. McKenna, as well as Research Associate Eric Delson.

Several outside firms played pivotal roles in the design, development, and production of this project. The person most responsible for helping to translate these scientific concepts into a three-dimensional exhibition is my colleague and friend, Ralph Appelbaum. Other key personnel at Ralph Appelbaum Associates included Melanie Ide, Miranda Smith, Francis O'Shea, Laura Genninger, Doug Balder, Elisabeth Cannell, Shari Berman, Chip Jeffries, and Evelyn Reilly; at Lehrer McGovern Bovis, Inc., key personnel included Peter Lehrer, Leslie Craig, David Reese, Sander Goldman, Robert Salpeter, Sandy Ginsberg, Greg Soder, and Joe Maraia; at Kevin Roche John Dinkeloo and Associates, key personnel included Kevin Roche, James Owens, and John Owen.

The production of the interactive computer programs was directed by C-Wave, including Chris Krueger, Amy Pertschuk, Mark O'Brien, and Marc Charnow. Paintings for the Timelines computer program are by Rob Barber. The video productions were developed in conjunction with The Chedd-Angier Production Company, including John Angier, Richard Lewis, and Jill Singer. Animations were produced under the direction of Hall Train Moving Pictures, including Peter May and Hall Train of Research Casting International.

Murals for the Archaeopteryx case and the early tetrapod area were painted by Steve Quinn of the Museum's Exhibition Department. Several of the fleshed-out models in the dinosaur halls were sculpted by Matt Smith. The mount of Eurhinodelphis was constructed by Connie Barut.

A tremendous amount of the credit for the success of this exhibition program should go to the Fossil Hall Renovation Group's administrators, preparators, and mount makers who labored daily on the project. Working together with them, I gleaned a lifetime's worth of insight about both paleontology and people in general. They have contributed a resource about evolutionary history that I hope they will take pride in for the rest of their lives. Among that staff I would like to pay special tribute to Melissa Posen, Associate Project Director, who was responsible for managing the dizzying array of day-to-day operations for this very complex undertaking. Also invaluable were the guidance and good nature of Richard Slawski, Director of Construction. At various times, we were aided with the administrative coordination and graphic research by Sarah Wilson, Dina Langis, Susan Illman, Gina Gould, Scott Sampson, Tracey Osborne, and Mary Potenciano. Most of the direct, hands-on work with the fossils was done by three supremely talented groups of artisans, including the Preparation Group, under the supervision of Jeanne Kelly; the Mount-making Group, under the supervision of Phillip Fraley; and the Installation Group, under the supervision of Steven Warsavage. I asked each of their crew members to list the three most meaningful tasks they had participated in. Here are their thoughts:

THE PREPARATION GROUP

David McCornack, Assistant Supervisor
- Plaque mount of *Paramys*, a primitive rodent
- Cast of *Diatryma*, a large flightless bird
- Preparation of *Edaphosaurus*, an early relative of mammals

Jane Mason, Preparator
- Preparation and painting of *Protohippus*, a three-toed horse
- Painting of *Heterodontosaurus*, an early relative of duckbills
- Preparation of *Triceratops*, a horned dinosaur

Marilyn Fox, Preparator
- Preparation of neck vertebrae of *Tyrannosaurus*, a large carnivorous dinosaur
- Molding and casting of embryo of oviraptorid, a small, beaked, carnivorous dinosaur
- Preparation of original mount and new skull of *Merychipppus,* a three-toed horse

Dennis Wilson, Preparator
- Sculpting of dinosaur bas-relief models for family tree
- Mount of *Mononykus*, a primitive, flightless bird
- Disassembly and preparation of *Tyrannosaurus*

Vito Cannella, Preparator
- Sculpting and fabrication of node models
- Preparation of *Tyrannosaurus*
- Fabrication of skull of *Barosaurus*, a giant herbivorous dinosaur

Ronald Clarke, Assistant Supervisor
- Mount of *Vulpavus*, a primitive carnivore
- Cast of *Obdurodon* skull, a primitive platypus

MOUNT-MAKING GROUP

Paul Zawisha, Assistant Supervisor
- Design and fabrication of armature for neck and tail of *Apatosaurus*, a giant herbivorous dinosaur
- Fabrication of armature for neck and tail of *Tyrannosaurus*
- Mount of *Ramoceros*, an early relative of antelope

Matthew Josephs, Mount-maker
- Mount of *Amphicyon*, an early relative of bears and dogs
- Armatures for neck and tail of *Apatosaurus*
- Fabrication of *Tyrannosaurus* model and armature

Dion Kliner, Mount-maker
- Disassembly and armature fabrication for mount of *Tyrannosaurus*
- Mount of *Buettneria*, a primitive tetrapod
- Mount of *Simosthenurus*, an early relative of kangaroos

Lawrence Lee, Mount-maker
- Fabrication of armature for neck and tail of *Apatosaurus*
- Remounting of *Tyrannosaurus*
- Mounting of elasmosaur, a long-necked, marine reptile

Richard Webber, Mount-maker
- Disassembly and armature fabrication for mount of *Tyrannosaurus*
- Fabrication of metal body outline for *Indricotherium*, a giant rhinoceros
- Fabrication of metal body outline for *Edaphosaurus*, an early relative of mammals

Jenny Lee, Mount-maker
- Fabrication of metal body outline for camels
- Disarticulation of *Tyrannosaurus* mount
- Armatures for mammal skulls

Steven Singer, Mount-maker
- Mount of *Prestosuchus*

INSTALLATION GROUP

Marc Mancini, Installation Preparator
- Fabrication of metal body outlines for horses
- Moving and installation of the *Apatosaurus* mount and trackway
- Crating and moving the mammoth and mastodon skeletons

John Fulton, Installation Preparator
- Base reconstruction for mounts of sloths, camels, and *Amphicyon*
- Moving and installation of the *Apatosaurus* mount and trackway

- Crating and moving of mammoth and mastodon skeletons

Carl Mehling, Installation Preparator
- Hanging of model and skeleton *Stupendemys*, a large turtle
- Installation of *Barosaurus* backbone
- Researching and installing *Triceratops* hips

Gerrard Gallagher, Installation Preparator
- Moving of *Apatosaurus* mount
- Moving of *Apatosaurus* trackway
- Crating and moving of mammoth and mastodon skeletons

This book was made possible in large part due to the encouragement and advice of my editor David Morton and to the extensive work on graphic research and photographic captions by Marilyn Fox. Also instrumental were the friendship and counseling of Sam Fleishman. Within the Museum, the efforts of Sigmund G. Ginsburg, Vice President for Business Development, Rena Zurofsky, and Scarlett Lovell aided the coordination of arrangements. The book's layout was designed by Abigail Sturges, and most of the images illustrate the photographic expertise of Denis Finnin, Scott Frances, Jackie Beckett, and Craig Chesek.

Above all, my own efforts in this project were sustained through the patient understanding, rejuvenating enthusiasm, and calming companionship of Elizabeth Chapman.

Lowell Dingus
December 1995

The grand Roosevelt Memorial Hall entrance to the Museum, facing Central Park West, during the first opening for the new mammal halls in 1994 as part of the Museum's 125th anniversary.

THE HALLS OF VERTEBRATE EVOLUTION

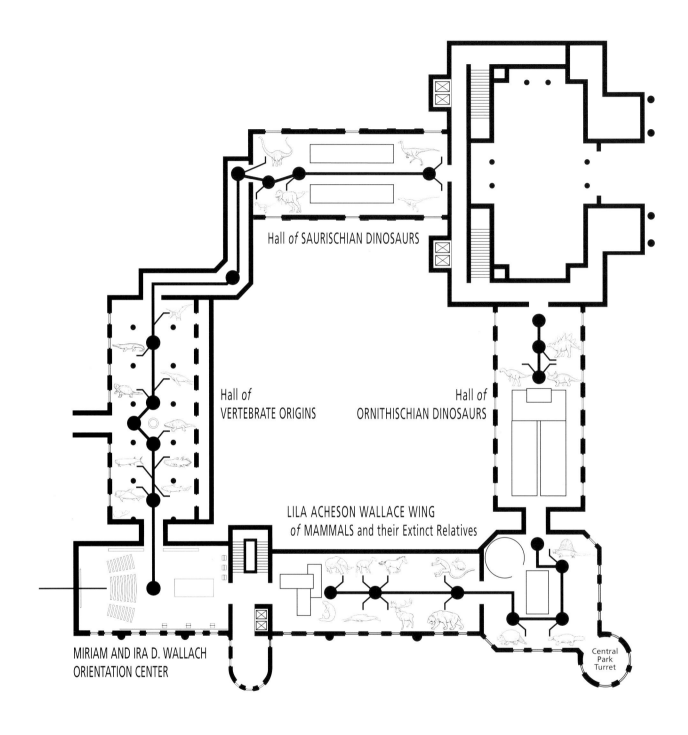

Hall of SAURISCHIAN DINOSAURS

Hall of
VERTEBRATE ORIGINS

Hall of
ORNITHISCHIAN DINOSAURS

LILA ACHESON WALLACE WING
of MAMMALS and their Extinct Relatives

MIRIAM AND IRA D. WALLACH
ORIENTATION CENTER

Central
Park
Turret

FOURTH FLOOR

*Floor plan for the six Halls of Vertebrate Evolution on the
fourth floor of the museum. The halls cover about 57,000
square feet, and the fossils are arranged along a gigantic
evolutionary tree for vertebrates.*

PREFACE

For generations, a visit to the dinosaur halls at the American Museum of Natural History has been a mandatory stop on any tour of New York. More than three million people a year visit the museum, and about half come to see the dinosaur halls. These exhibits represent a cornerstone for both the museum's public image and its educational mission: each year they provide around 500,000 students with their first face-to-face introduction to their evolutionary heritage.

Since the dinosaur exhibitions were last renovated forty years ago, that cornerstone has deteriorated. Although most of the fossil mounts were still structurally sound, the information was woefully outdated. Most ten-year-olds knew that we had the wrong skull on our *"Brontosaurus."* In fact, they also knew it should not be called *"Brontosaurus"* at all but rather *Apatosaurus.*

In 1986 the museum began planning an extensive program to renovate and reorganize these popular halls. By the time this six-year, $48 million construction project is completed, I will have spent a decade working exclusively on it.

To be sure, I have always wanted to be a paleontologist. There was no doubt about that from the first grade on. The romance of collecting and studying fossils represented an irresistible attraction. It still does. As a child, I imagined myself following in the footsteps of famed explorer and naturalist Roy Chapman Andrews to collect dinosaurs in the Gobi Desert, but as a student at the University of California, the last thing I imagined myself doing was building museum exhibitions. Like most people, I had no idea what was involved. At the interview for my first job after graduation, I was told that the position would entail doing an exhibit on evolution at the California Academy of Sciences. I naively pictured myself installing a few fossils in some new exhibit cases. What could be more simple? I certainly never imagined spending a large part of my career involved in such activities.

Little did I realize that my undergraduate degree in geology and graduate degrees in geology and paleontology would barely begin to prepare me for directing a full-scale exhibition. Such projects involve assorted personalities ranging from architects and lawyers to exhibit designers and curators. Accordingly, the issues that must be addressed run the gamut from restoring architectural landmarks built in the last century to reconstructing 150 million-year-old animals that no one has ever seen.

I suspect that directing a full-scale museum exhibition is somewhat analogous to helping conceptualize, design, and develop a major production on Broadway. A budget must be set and monitored. The inside of the theater must be prepared with an eye for both aesthetics and safety. Props must be conceived and constructed. A script must be written, edited, and reviewed by a diverse set of advisors. The cast of characters must be identified, assembled, and prepared for the presentation. Funders must be consulted and updated. It does not just happen overnight. A wide range of competing perspectives and influences must be discussed and balanced. To me, that process has been the most interesting and challenging aspect of this undertaking.

This book presents an overview of the whole exhibition project, all seven halls, covering about 65,000 square feet of the largest private natural history museum in the world. We address not only the themes and specimens in the halls but also the organizational structure and decision-making process. We review the early phases of planning and design, the architectural intent, the construction of the immense new *Barosaurus* mount in the landmark Roosevelt Memorial Hall, and the concepts behind the exhibition in the Miriam and Ira D. Wallach Orientation Center. We describe the restoration of Calvert Vaux's original exhibition hall, which now contains exhibits about the origin of the major vertebrate groups, and the work involved in bringing our *Apatosaurus* mount up to current paleontological code in the Hall of Saurischian Dinosaurs. We journey back 300 million years to explore our own evolutionary roots in the Lila Acheson Wallace Wing of Mammals and Their Extinct Relatives. Along the way, we encounter many exceptional fossils, such as the exquisitely "mummified" duckbill in the Hall of Ornithischian Dinosaurs, that provide windows into the lives of individual animals that lived millions and even hundreds of millions of years ago, and we meet many talented scientists, preparators, mount-makers, and artists who have helped revive this long-lost evolutionary story.

In addition to providing the community with a stimulating scientific resource on evolutionary history, another extremely important aspect of the renovation was the decision to utilize the long-obscured original architecture of the exhibition halls. Our goal has been to marry the world's best collection of dinosaurs and other fossil vertebrates with some of the most spectacular exhibition galleries in New York. The museum complex includes some of the most treasured architectural landmarks in the region, and we made an early commitment to restore these spaces and the specimens in them to come as close to their original grandeur as possible. This approach is in stark contrast to that now taken in most museums, where natural light is eliminated from exhibitions and casts rather than real fossils are used.

Beyond that, the project has taken place during a pivotal period in the history of museums as institutions. Funding is scarce; competition for resources is fierce. Given present economic and social needs, many museum professionals are openly debating what role museums should play in society. Should exhibitions be sources of public entertainment or of education? How might they help reverse the trend toward scientific illiteracy so prevalent among both students and the general public? Is it enough simply to discuss what visitors want to know about, or do exhibitions have a responsibility to broaden their audiences' horizons by presenting more challenging information? All these issues have had a profound effect on the development of this project, and in turn, the development of the project, as well as the exhibitions themselves, provides a mirror for us to reflect upon both our social values and our position within the evolutionary sequence of life on Earth.

*These imposing mounts
of a mammoth (left), a
mastodon (right), and a
gomphothere (behind),
are fossil relatives of
living elephants; they
guard the exit from the
mammal halls.*

INTRODUCTION:
THE EARLY PLANNING

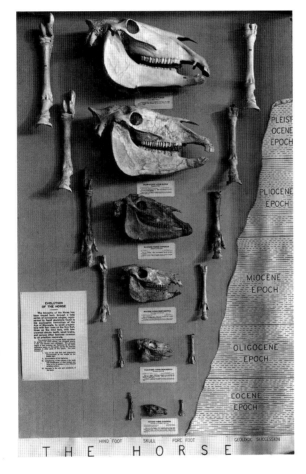

One of the exhibits from the old mammal halls showed a simplified picture of horse evolution arranged in chronologic order from the oldest fossil at the bottom to the more recent forms at the top.

When I first joined the Exhibition Department at the American Museum of Natural History in 1987, the museum was planning to renovate only one of the fossil halls on the fourth floor: the Osborn Hall of Late Mammals, named after Henry Fairfield Osborn, founder of the museum's Department of Vertebrate Paleontology. The exhibits included the original, classic display of horse evolution, assembled back in the early 1900s by Osborn and his influential student William Diller Matthew. But over the decades, the hall had deteriorated extensively. The carpet was badly worn, and one side of the exhibition hall had even been boarded up because so many specimens had been removed from their cases for scientific study and never returned. Clearly, something needed to be done, if only on account of the dilapidated image of the museum that this exhibit conveyed to the public.

Working with the museum's administration, the outside design firm of Ralph Appelbaum Associates, and the curators in the Department of Vertebrate Paleontology under the direction of Michael Novacek, we spent two years planning a renovation. A small group of us took trips to recently opened fossil exhibitions at the British Museum in London, the Senckenberg Museum in Frankfurt, the Museum am Lowentor in Stuttgart, the Royal Tyrrell Museum outside Calgary, the California Academy of Sciences in San Francisco, the Smithsonian Institution in Washington, and the Philadelphia Academy of Sciences. This sampling of contemporary paleontological exhibitions exposed us to a wide variety of intellectual approaches and design styles. Some, like the new exhibitions in the British Museum, were highly interactive and intellectually innovative, even to the point of dealing with a new approach for establishing evolutionary relationships called cladistics (see pages 40–41 for an explanation of this concept). Others, such as the new museum in Stuttgart, were stylistically influential in annealing stark stone flooring with minimalistic metal and glass casework.

This survey of contemporary exhibitions helped our planning group focus on the fundamental issue: to what extent would our new exhibition present substantial scientific information reflecting the research going on in our museum, and to what extent would it be driven by the need to entertain our visitors in order to raise attendance and revenues? Whereas some institutions rely heavily on easy-to-understand, anecdotal labels and robotic recreations of extinct dinosaurs that appeal to the lowest common denominator of visitor intellect, others strive for more elegant and classical presentations featuring more technical scientific information. For us, this was not necessarily an either/or situation; the battle lay in how to best balance these two competing influences.

In our first fully developed plan and model, we decided to explore a novel approach that strongly reflected our institution's research activities and unparalleled collections of vertebrate fossils. In mounting exhibits on evolutionary history, there are two basic organizational options: chronological and genealogical. Most museums choose to develop a chronologically based "walk-through-time" that begins with specimens and dioramas of the earliest known fauna and flora, then continues up to the most recent. During my initial discussions with the exhibition designer, however, we agreed that we should try to set this exhibition apart from all the others. Not that the walk-through-time approach is a bad way to present evolutionary history. It is perfectly fine, and if done well, it can convey an important sense of how the Earth's fauna and flora have changed over the vast expanse of geologic time. But we determined to do it differently.

The breakthrough in our thinking came early in our discussions. Instead of organizing our exhibition chronologically, I proposed to organize it around the evolutionary relationships of the animals in the hall. It occurred to us that most people are fascinated by their own family history, especially in a country of immigrants like the United States, where a person's roots often extend back into another continent within just a few generations. Banking on this natural curiosity rooted in kinship, we decided to design a framework that would extend one's own family history out to include our other mammalian cousins because evolutionary history is, in a very real sense, simply an extrapolation of one's own genealogical history.

The exhbition designer Ralph Appelbaum and I decided to approach the curators and the administration with a plan based on the motif of an evolutionary tree. A main path down the center of the hall served as the trunk of the tree, and branches off of it led to smaller subgalleries that contained closely related animals belonging to different orders of mammals, such as whales or elephants. Much of the research in the Department of Vertebrate Paleontology focuses on trying to establish the evolutionary relationships among different vertebrate groups. In fact, during the last two decades, the museum has played a critical role in developing and promoting cladistics, a new method, for deciphering evolutionary kinship. We wanted to use the museum's exceptionally diverse collection of fossil mammals, featuring everything from cave bears to mammoths to "Irish elk," to illustrate cladistics and help the public understand how the modern mammalian fauna evolved. In this way, we could provide the public with a unique perspective and resource about evolutionary history and, at the same time, distinguish our presentation from all the other evolutionary exhibitions.

Before we got much further, a change in the museum's administration catalyzed a radical reevaluation of the project's scope. The new president, George D. Langdon, and the director, William J. Moynihan, posed a seemingly simple question at our first meeting: should we renovate just one hall of fossil mammals, or should we develop plans to renovate all the halls of fossil vertebrates, including dinosaurs? I was stunned and somewhat intimidated. When I had interviewed for my position, the possibility was mentioned that once we renovated Osborn Hall, we might go on to renovate the other halls, one by one. But four at once? The only projects of comparable scale in the museum world involve building a new museum from scratch. I did not expect anyone to give serious consideration to such an expensive and large-scale project, but what I was only remotely aware of was that the renovation would actually be less expensive than an alternative project being considered, which actually was for an entirely new wing along Columbus Avenue.

Thus in 1988, our planning team, including the exhibition designers, curators in vertebrate paleontology, and key administrators, regrouped to begin evaluating the possibilities and costs of renovating all four fossil halls on the fourth floor, including the two halls of fossil mammals, the halls of early and late dinosaurs, and a small fossil fish alcove. The first several months were spent developing a concept based on cladistics, our approach for Osborn Hall, that could be extended throughout the other halls. A group of experts in paleontology and exhibitions was asked to come in to consult with us, and these initial studies pointed up two critical issues, one physical and the other conceptual.

The four exhibition halls on the fourth floor were designed to tell the evolutionary story of vertebrates, so we were not changing the scientific scope of the exhibition. But the major flaw in the old halls was that there was no way to get visitors up to the start of the story: the very small treatment of fish and amphibian evolution was relegated to a dead end at the back of the Early Dinosaur Hall. To solve this problem, an architectural firm with a long history of work in large museums—Kevin Roche John Dinkeloo and Associates—was brought in. We decided that the best way to solve this problem was to solve another critical problem at the same time; which was that our library had run out of space. These two problems were connected because the library was adjacent to the Early Dinosaur Hall, and if we could find a new place for it within the museum's complex of twenty-three interconnected buildings, we could develop a continuous loop of six halls by connecting the four existing fossil halls to the old library space and the old Earth History Hall. In all, the plan would involve the renovation of 65,000 square feet of exhibition space in seven halls and the construction of a new 50,000-square-foot library complex. The new library was scheduled to open in 1992, the two mammal halls in 1994, and the two dinosaur halls in 1995. The Hall of Vertebrate Origins and the Orientation Center could not open until after we finished the new library, so they were slated for completion in 1996.

The museum's Exhibition Department was already engaged in the construction of a new Hall of Human Evolution and Human Biology, as well as in the installation of numerous large temporary exhibitions. Consequently, a new department of twenty people was established within the museum to work exclusively on the fossil hall project. To oversee its development and production, a select steering committee of the museum's Board of Trustees was convened. Working in concert with the full board of trustees, a budget of $43.8 million was originally established. Finally, to keep other departments within the museum abreast of issues and developments involving the project, an in-house steering committee was established under the supervision of the museum's director, William J. Moynihan. And in essence, excluding some games of musical chairs among the personnel, this represents the scope of the project.

1 THE BAIT IN THE BIG TANK: **THE *BAROSAURUS***

The great 110-foot height of the Roosevelt Memorial Hall provided an impressive space in which to build a new dinosaur mount. Here, an Allosaurus (right) attacks a juvenile Barosaurus (left) as the mother (middle) rises to defend her young.

MOUNT IN ROOSEVELT MEMORIAL HALL

Barosaurus is one of the largest dinosaurs ever known to have walked the Earth. Our specimen, the most complete skeleton known for the genus, was discovered by the legendary collector Earl Douglass about 1912 in the badlands of the Morrison Formation that now make up Dinosaur National Monument near Vernal, Utah. But from the moment it was decided to exhibit this creature in our main entrance hall facing Central Park, the *Barosaurus* mount has played the role of "problem child" for our renovation—but not necessarily in a bad way. And its checkered past extends back far beyond this exhibition project.

When our preliminary planning for the renovations was completed in 1989, we asked several consultants to review our ideas; among them was an irrepressible exhibit designer from California named Gordon Ashby. After spending a couple of days reviewing preliminary plans, we asked him what he thought. He remarked that we had a spectacular collection of fossils to exhibit and that we would clearly have no trouble incorporating a lot of scientific substance into the exhibition. But he still foresaw one problem:

"What's that," I asked.

"Where's the big tank?" he replied.

"What do you mean?" I asked, completely baffled.

"Oh," he said, "you know, after you buy your ticket to go into the aquarium, the first thing you do is walk over to the information desk and ask, 'Where's the big tank?'"

I have often wondered if he realizes that he catalyzed the construction of the tallest freestanding dinosaur mount in the world.

Our *Barosaurus* lived about 140 million years ago along the flood plain of a shallow continental sea that stretched from the Gulf of Mexico up toward the Arctic Ocean. Yet despite its size, this immense herbivore was actually rather gracile. With its elongated neck and whiplike tail, it stretched about ninety feet in length but may have weighed only between ten and fifteen tons. Based on the paucity of specimens found, it is considered to be one of the rarest sauropods, the group that includes the largest long-necked dinosaurs.

When Earl Douglass and his field crews were carrying out their excavation between 1912 and 1914, Douglass first thought that the specimen belonged to the genus *Diplodocus,* one of the more commonly preserved sauropods, so he apparently did not recognize the specimen's scientific significance. Consequently, he used the specimen to help fill in the gaps that existed in various mounts of *Diplodocus* in other museums. A section of the tail went to the Carnegie Museum in Pittsburgh; a section of the neck went to the Smithsonian Institution in Washington, D.C.; and the rest stayed closer to its home at the University of Utah. Subsequently, it was established that the skeleton represented an individual of *Barosaurus,* not *Diplodocus;* as a result, the other museums could not use the acquired sections in their mounts.

More than a decade passed. Enter Barnum Brown, probably the most famous of all the great dinosaur collectors. In 1929, after traveling to most of the major museums in the United States to assess their collections of dinosaur fossils, Brown realized that the three partial skeletons actually

FOSSIL HORSE TRADING

The following confidential memorandum from the archives of the American Museum of Natural History provides details on some of the exchanges that brought the widely dispersed Barosaurus *skeleton to the American Museum:*

REPORT ON *BAROSAURUS*

Supplementing my report of July 26, 1929. I again visited Salt Lake City in December and secured the following agreement from Dr. [Frederick J.] Pack who has authority from the President and Trustees of the University to act in their behalf in this negotiation.

Value of specimen agreed upon $5000. Terms $2,500 in cash, balance in trade.

Specimens desired by University of Utah: a three-toed horse skeleton (we can supply a composite skeleton), and other mammal material to make up difference. American Museum to box, ship and pay transportation charges on *Barosaurus.*

This agreement I consider fair with full value coming to the American Museum providing we can secure the remainder of this skeleton.

The part of this *Barosaurus* skeleton in the National Museum consists of the last ten cervical vertebrae with ribs; three anterior dorsals; left scapula and humerus. It has cost $3,400 to clean and restore it (Laboratory records).

[Charles W.] Gilmore (confidentially) favors an exchange and desires a free mountable skeleton of *Gorgosaurus.* Dr. [Alexander] Wetmore does not favor disposal of this *Barosaurus* neck (from conversation reported by Gilmore).

American Museum can offer the following specimen in exchange: *Gorgosaurus* No. 5434. Skull and jaws, all cervicals, and dorsal vertebrae, all ribs, forelimbs, one femur. Sacrum, hind limbs, except one femur, will be cast.

Cost of preparing and casting hind limbs and part of tail $4,123. To finish tail and sacrum $450.—total cost $4,573. (Cost taken from Laboratory time sheets and exclusive of collecting and transportation charges).

The caudal series of this skeleton nine or ten vertebrae in the Carnegie Museum are preserved in two blocks, 348/A and 349/B according to their quarry charts.

So far no negotiations have been undertaken to secure this part of the specimen.

A.M.N.H.
Dec. 31, 1929

Barnum Brown

AMNH

Bone collector Barnum Brown and his wife, Lilian, at Howe Quarry in 1934

Facing page: Roosevelt Memorial Hall, pictured here before the renovation and the addition of the huge Barosaurus *display, is a major entrance on Central Park West. It has been designated an Interior City Landmark.*

A little horse trading was required in order to get a specimen impressive enough to fill Roosevelt Memorial Hall. Sections of the Barosaurus *skeleton came to the American Museum of Natural History from three different museums in exchange for other fossil specimens.*

Facing page:
The charging Allosaurus
threatens the young
Barosaurus *in Roosevelt*
Memorial Hall.

The young Barosaurus
peeks around the adult,
which rears protectively.

represented the remains of a single individual.

Speaking independently to representatives from each of the three museums, Brown negotiated deals for all three sections of the *Barosaurus* skeleton. A memorandum in the museum's archives details the terms for two of these deals: the University of Utah wanted $2500, the skeleton of a fossil three-toed horse, and other mammal material, whereas the Smithsonian, against the better judgment of one of their most influential curators, wanted a mountable skeleton of the large carnivorous dinosaur then called *Gorgosaurus* (now called *Albertosaurus*). In the end, the American Museum of Natural History gained title to one of the most unusual dinosaur fossils in existence without having to excavate a single grain of sand.

Although some plans were initiated to build a mount in the early 1950s, four more decades passed before the museum actually decided what to do with the skeleton. To announce this latest renovation of the fossil halls, the administration asked us if we had any specimens that we might be able to use for a dinosaur mount in the Roosevelt Memorial Hall. This enormous hall, with its gigantic columns and spacious barrel vault studded with plaster rosettes, was designed by John Russell Pope who also designed the National Gallery of Art and the Jefferson Memorial in Washington, D.C. The initial planning for its construction commenced immediately after the death of Theodore Roosevelt on 6 January 1919. In 1931 Franklin D. Roosevelt, then governor of New York, laid the cornerstone, and later on 19 January 1936, as president he dedicated the massive monument. The hall extends over 8,000 square feet. To us, it seemed like we had plenty of room to do something momentous of our own—but what?

After some reflection, it occurred to me that the most spectacular thing to do would be to mount a gigantic sauropod rearing up on its hind legs; I thought, however, that I would have no chance of convincing the curator then in charge of the dinosaur collections, Eugene Gaffney, to undertake such a project. Even more than I, he was known for his disdain of such speculative "dinomania." I was totally dumbfounded when he came to me a few days later with the suggestion that we mount the *Barosaurus* skeleton stored in the basement in a pose that would show the animal rearing up on its hind limbs. Shortly thereafter, a new curator of the dinosaur collections, Mark Norell, arrived to take up his position at the museum. Much to my continuing amazement, Norell, who looks as unkindly as Gaffney does on behavioral speculations about dinosaurs, immediately jumped in. Together they conjured up the idea of a herd of barosaurs being chased through the hall by a pack of allosaurs. Clearly, I'd been completely out-flanked. But fortunately there just was not enough room, even in the ample confines of the Roosevelt Memorial Hall, to stage such an epic event. We finally settled on a somewhat simpler scenario: We would mount one rearing adult barosaur protecting her baby from the onslaught of an attacking allosaur.

In addition to the physical problems and risks involved in building such a mount, there were intellectual risks. *Barosaurus* characteristically walked on all four legs. Fossil trackways, like the one exhibited in the Hall of Saurischian Dinosaurs behind our *Apatosaurus* mount, document this

In this reconstruction by Charles R. Knight an Apatosaurus *rises up to nibble some soft new leaves at the top of a tree.*

without any doubt. Nonetheless, the idea of a sauropod rearing up momentarily on its hind legs was not a novel idea, although no one had ever been foolish enough to attempt a freestanding mount. Back in the early 1900s, the first accomplished paleontological artist, Charles R. Knight, had worked with Osborn to illustrate *Apatosaurus* rearing up on its hind legs to feed on vegetation high in the trees. Yet it is important to state that the point of our mount was not to defend the accuracy of this rearing posture. We had two other objectives in mind.

First, we needed a new star to feature in our "big tank." Coincidentally, the Roosevelt Memorial Hall, which has been designated an Interior City Landmark, was scheduled for renovation during the first two years of design development for The Halls of Vertebrate Evolution. What better place could one ask for to create a powerful new symbol for announcing the renovation? In fact, under its towering 110-foot barrel-vaulted ceiling we could have stuck in two barosaurs, one on top of the other, and still had room to spare.

Second, and more importantly, we wanted to take this opportunity to introduce a major theme that could be drawn out in the exhibitions upstairs on the fourth floor: What do we know and what do we not know about these long-extinct dinosaurs? There are a multitude of intriguing questions regarding dinosaurs that remain unresolved. Yet, because they are like monsters-come-true, dinosaurs stimulate intense curiosity and interest in people of all ages. We want to know everything about them. Unfortunately, the fossils do not provide unequivocal evidence to answer many questions we wonder about. This is hard to accept, whether you hold a Ph.D. in paleontology or are a more casual but fascinated observer.

Although the fossils are good for telling us how large these dinosaurs were and which ones were close evolutionary cousins, they do not tell us much about how extinct dinosaurs behaved. Could *Barosaurus* rear up? In truth, we just do not know, and we took great care to state this directly in the exhibit labels and promotional materials. There is some evidence to suggest that the animal's center of gravity was located back near the hips, which would have made it easier to lift the front part of the body. Some of the tail vertebrae even have struts on the bottom that may represent supports for when the animal used its tail while rearing. And most large terrestrial animals use an approach to reproduction that involves the male assuming a reared-up posture by resting its front legs on the back of the female.

But could the barosaur's hind legs and hips really have borne all that weight, and could it have pumped blood up to the head when it was fifty feet off the ground? One cardiologist even went so far as to propose in print that the animal may have needed eight extra hearts, placed in four pairs along the neck, to pump blood all the way up to the head when the animal raised itself to its full extent. Given that no other vertebrate has more than one heart, we viewed this proposal with extreme skepticism. Giraffes, which have the longest necks of any living creature, do have an enormous twenty-five pound heart, along with specialized muscles in the neck to help propel blood up to the brain. Were barosaurs similar? Again, we do not really know because we cannot dissect one or go out and observe *Barosaurus* in the wilds of the Jurassic. Furthermore, we have no information about what color the animal was; only rarely do fossils preserve an impression of the animal's skin, which tells us what it felt like but nothing about its color.

With our ideas and concepts pulled together, now all we had to do was find someone foolhardy enough to help us build the mount. Since we were just beginning to assemble a mount-making crew of our own at the museum, we decided to go outside. After seeking recommendations from other paleontological colleagues, in through our door walked the unassuming figure of Peter May, a former mount-maker at the Royal Tyrrell Museum in Alberta. Although he was only thirty-five at the time, his easy-going attitude, mixed with his confident approach to the structural and logistic problems involved, quickly convinced us that he was our man. While working as a preparator at the Royal Ontario Museum in Toronto, he had started a company of his own to build dinosaur mounts on contract for other museums. So his staff was anxious for a chance to make its mark.

In the fall of 1990, May and his crew drove a semi-truck across the Canadian-U.S. border and arrived at the doorstep of the museum to pick up the massive, yet delicate, bones of the barosaur skeleton. From there, the peripatetic barosaur took off once more on a year-long sabbatical from its basement abode to be molded and cast at May's shop in Toronto. The reason for the casting was simple: each large neck vertebra of the adult barosaur weighs about 150 pounds. Consequently, the real bones of the skeleton would have been much too heavy to use in a freestanding mount in which the neck stretched vertically from about twenty-five feet up to almost fifty feet in the air. As a result, light-weight fiberglass and urethane replicas of the real bones would be made and mounted on the internal steel framework or armature. The armature itself relied on a suitably ancient scheme of engineering, the tripod. To show the animal rearing up on its hind limbs would obviously require a stable base: the columnar legs would provide two struts and the sturdy tail of the animal would supply the third.

After six or seven months of casting and welding, May called to arrange for the barosaur's debut to be held in the somewhat-less-than-opulent surroundings of the parking lot behind his shop. Not knowing quite what to expect, a group of us from the museum flew up to see the show. As always, May was humorously relaxed and confident, having rented a crane and a fifty-foot lift to aid in the assembly. The day dawned brilliantly, and a small crowd, including a television crew, some photographers, and even a "spy" from another museum, assembled to witness the resurrection. Slowly the tripod was pieced together in modules attached to the pelvis. Next the ribcage was lifted into place on top of the tripod. Finally, the three sections of the neck were ready to be erected. Nervously pacing around the parking lot, we watched the first section extend up more than thirty feet; the second ascended to around forty feet; and the third topped out at almost fifty feet.

Although the size was undeniably intimidating, the strangest thing was that the mount actually looked rather natural and graceful, a result that I had been afraid to expect.

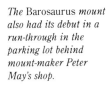

In an outdoor run-through, the charging Allosaurus *is seen for the first time.*

The Barosaurus *mount also had its debut in a run-through in the parking lot behind mount-maker Peter May's shop.*

A cherry picker is used in Roosevelt Memorial Hall to put the finishing touches on the Barosaurus *mount as the soaring head looks on.*

Facing page: *Each of the real* Barosaurus *neck bones weighs about 150 punds, but the cast bones weigh only about 5 pounds each.*

Ironically, even though I had helped to promote the project, I too had always been extremely skeptical about whether sauropods could rear up to such heights, but the grace of the mount almost erased my doubt.

Peter May needed about six more months to put the finishing touches on the three animals in the scene. In fact, the engineering problems associated with posing the allosaur charging on one foot were much more demanding of May's talents than building the barosaur, and sculpting all the missing pieces of the juvenile sauropod, which was based only on a partial neck and skull in the museum's collection and on some limb bones from the collection at Dinosaur National Monument, was another time-consuming enterprise. This whole process was aided greatly by the patient advice of the world's foremost expert on sauropods, Jack McIntosh. Finally in November 1991, the barosaur was ready to return to the museum.

The trip home and the early phases of the assembly went smoothly but hoisting the neck to the top of the ribcage provided some anxious moments. Instead of putting on the neck in sections, May thought it best to weld the three pieces together and lift it into place as one unit, a kind of all-or-nothing approach that seemed appropriate to this project. The whole neck, however, proved to be quite unwieldy and difficult to maneuver. Using straps attached to both ends, May hoisted it horizontally up to the full extent of the fifty-foot lift. He then had to rotate the neck from its horizontal position into a more vertical position that would allow it to slip into the armature at the top of the ribcage. As word spread through the museum that the neck was being assembled, a crowd of about one hundred staff members gathered to watch. For almost two hours, we wrestled with the 140-million-year-old giant. As May pulled and twisted the neck from above with the straps, we yanked on the top of the ribcage from below, trying to get the neck armature to slip into place. It was as if the barosaur preferred not to rear up again, whether or not it could have done so when it was alive. It had performed its trick once, in Toronto, and that was more than enough as far as it was concerned. Finally the neck slipped into place with an abrupt thud, and a round of relieved applause echoed throughout the hall. With sparks streaming down toward the base as the neck was welded onto the ribcage, we figured most of the excitement was over.

But on 29 November 1991 (the day after Thanksgiving), as I was walking to the subway on my way to the museum to help complete the installation of the mount, I stepped into a local newspaper shop and looked down at the front page of a local daily. An instantaneous surge of adrenaline coursed through my body. I simply could not believe it. Someone had bit the bait in the "big tank."

On the front page was an image that we had commissioned a prominent paleontological artist, John Gurche, to paint. It depicted a fleshed-out, color portrait of the barosaur, with the allosaur charging in from the shadows to try and make a meal of the baby cowering behind its mother. The headline read,: "What's Wrong With This Picture?" I knew immediately what was "wrong."

The newspaper had called several prominent paleontologists to elicit their opinions on the accuracy of the

museum's mount. Understandably, most were skeptical, as they should have been. The subhead on the front page read: "Experts: Museum Wrong, Barosaurus Couldn't Stand Up." Inadvertently, they had played right into our hand. To us, the mount represents a kind of benignly baited hook. If visitors walk in, love the mount, and are inspired to learn more, we have succeeded. But if they walk in, and look up in disbelief, we have succeeded even more because any legitimate scientific analysis requires a healthy dose of skepticism.

But even with the public opening in early December behind us, our work on the barosaur mount was not yet quite complete. When the neck was lifted horizontally to begin installing it on top of the ribcage, the steel armature had bent where the strap was attached. As a result, the neck appeared to have a small kink in it even though it was not very noticeable. The more we looked at it, the more it bothered us. After a few weeks we talked it over with Peter May and decided to try to fix it.

The plan was simple in concept. We would remove a few neck vertebrae, cut out the bent segment of the metal armature, and splice in a new section of steel rod to smooth out the kink. The work was to begin after the museum closed for the day and continue through the night.

At first, things went smoothly. Two lifts were required. One lift held two of May's staff who worked at the level of the kink, while the other extended up to the skull, where two other workers steadied the whole neck. The fiberglass vertebrae were easily sawed off, and the kinked segment of steel tubing that ran up through the neck was cut out. A new piece of steel rod, about three feet long, was inserted into the steel tubing and welded into place. It was time to see if it worked.

As May's two young assistants began to let go of the neck, the barosaur leaned toward the front entrance. We were expecting some deflection in this direction, but we were not expecting what happened next. As the men let out more line, the neck continued to bend out and down toward the side of the hall. The articulations between adjacent neck vertebrae began to pop and snap all the way down the neck to the hips. It was as if the barosaur had requested the assistance of a modern chiropractor to correct a misalignment in its spine that had been bothering it since the Jurassic. For a brief moment, I watched the tallest free-standing dinosaur mount in the world become the tallest free-falling dinosaur mount. May and I yelled to the men in the upper bucket to pull in the slack on the strap attached to the top of the neck, but they seemed oblivious to what was happening. After several more confused and panic-filled moments, they finally responded and pulled the neck back up where it belonged.

The weight of the metal segment that we added had been enough to throw the whole neck out of balance. We therefore shortened the segment to reduce its weight and repaired a few spot welds that had been broken. The barosaur mount was finally completed, and our "problem child" has behaved well ever since.

2 THE OPENING ACT: **THE MIRIAM AND**

IRA D. WALLACH ORIENTATION CENTER

In the old Hall of the Age of Man, which now houses the Miriam and Ira D. Wallach Orientation Center, a row of mastodons and mammoths are surrounded by murals painted by Charles R. Knight in the early 1900s.

FOURTH FLOOR PLAN

On the fourth floor of the second building constructed at the museum, one entire hall·is dedicated to helping prepare visitors and students for their experience in the exhibition. This building, designed by the architects Cady, Berg, and See, was completed in 1891. At the same time, the museum hired Henry Fairfield Osborn to start a Department of Vertebrate Paleontology, and Osborn initiated plans to fill the hall with fossil mammals. He was keenly interested in the evolution of our own species and christened this gallery the Hall of the Age of Man, although the hall also contained specimens and information about other forms of mammalian life during the Ice Ages. A series of huge murals rimmed the perimeter walls just below the ceiling. These striking images were painted in the early 1900s by Charles R. Knight, and in addition to images depicting Osborn's view of early human evolution, the murals featured Pleistocene mammals in Siberia, California, and New Jersey. Until the 1930s, the hall contained some of the most impressive skeletons in the museum's collections, including the mammoths and mastodons. When the Hall of the Age of Man was demolished in the early 1960s, its space was converted into the Earth History Hall, and the Knight murals were removed from its walls and stored in the old Hall of Early Mammals. During the removal process many murals were extensively damaged, but our renovation project funded a two-year restoration program so that several could again be used for exhibition. When the mammal halls opened in 1994, the restored murals took their rightful place in the Hall of Advanced Mammals.

As part of the latest renovation, the new Orientation Center has been designed to introduce the major themes and structure of our exhibition. Visitors enter a spacious assembly area before beginning their journey through the halls. We plan to have them greeted by a fleshed-out model of a juvenile barosaur that expands on the theme introduced by the mount downstairs: what do we really know about these long-extinct animals? As the juvenile barosaur gazes on the visitor, a short accompanying video would explain that fossils like those of the *Barosaurus* are so spectacular that our natural curiosity leads us to want to know everything about them. But what do the fossils really tell us, and what mysteries remain unresolved?

One thing is certain; the fossils provide us with a fairly accurate idea about how large the living animal was. The tremendous size difference between the neck bones of the adult and of the juvenile barosaur clearly makes this point. The shapes of the bones tell us that *Barosaurus* was a closer cousin of other large, plant-eating sauropods than was the meat-eating *Allosaurus* because the bones of the allosaur, especially the arm bones, for example, look very different. We learn that fossil trackways, formed when a sauropod walked across an ancient mud flat, even show that animals like *Barosaurus* usually walked around on all four legs.

There are nevertheless, many intriguing questions about how *Barosaurus* behaved that the fossils just do not help us answer. The fossils do not provide any information about what color *Barosaurus* was. It may have had a dull skin color, or it may have had a brilliantly striking color pattern. We have no good evidence from the fossils about what kind

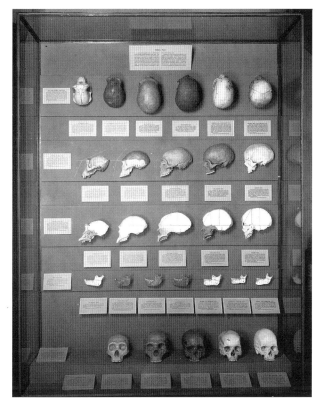

A wall exhibit from the old Hall of the Age of Man. Henry Fairfield Osborn, who started the Museum's Department of Vertebrate Paleontology in 1891, thought that this exhibit illustrated steps in his concept of human evolution.

In the Hall of the Age of Man, a Charles R. Knight mural of Ice Age wooly mammoths hung above the mount of Mammuthus, *a huge mammoth that lived 21,000 years ago.*

DEVONIAN PERIOD

Top: The muddy estuary of Escuminac Bay, in Quebec, Canada, 370 million years ago was the home of such fish as Eusthenopteron, *a lobe-finned fish;* Bothriolepis, *a placoderm; and* Scaumenacia, *a*

EOCENE EPOCH

Bottom: Fifty million years ago the margin of a large freshwater lake in the Green River area of Wyoming and Utah offered a diverse habitat for turtles such as Baena *and crocodiles such as*

JURASSIC PERIOD

Top: This painting represents the environment and extinct dinosaurs, such as Barosaurus and Allosaurus, of 140 million years ago in the Morrison Formation, a series of ancient rock beds now exposed throughout Utah, Colorado, and Wyoming.

CRETACEOUS PERIOD

Bottom: A representation of a scene from 107 million years ago in the Cloverly Formation, an area that extends through present-day Montana and Wyoming, shows an attack by Deinonychus.

Hall of VERTEBRATE ORIGINS

Halls of DINOSAURS

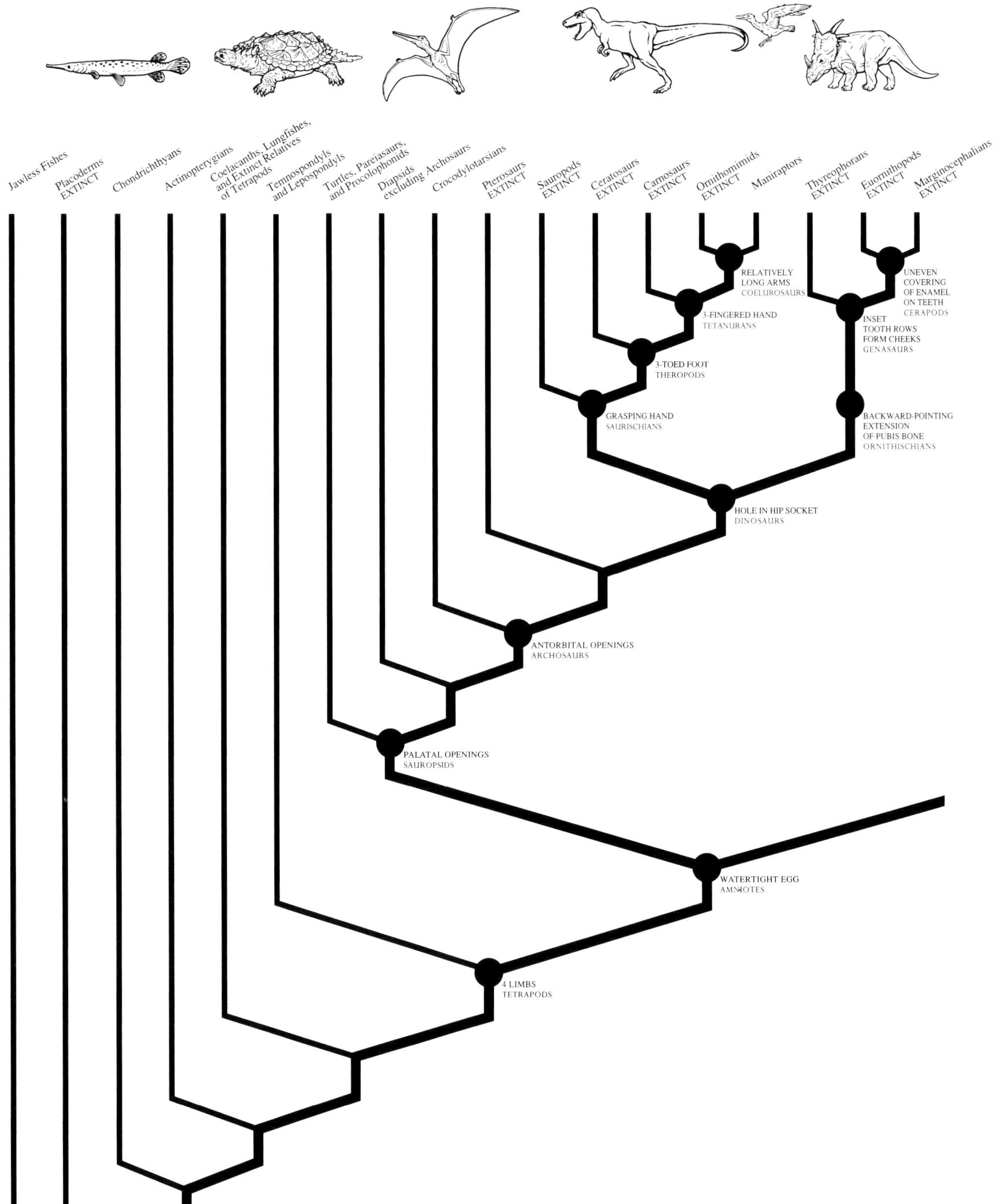

Jawless Fishes

Placoderms
EXTINCT

Chondrichthyans

Actinopterygians

Coelacanths, Lungfishes,
and Extinct Relatives
of Tetrapods

Temnospondyls
and Lepospondyls

Turtles, Pareiasaurs,
and Procolophonids

Diapsids
excluding Archosaurs

Crocodylotarsians

Pterosaurs
EXTINCT

Sauropods
EXTINCT

Ceratosaurs
EXTINCT

Carnosaurs
EXTINCT

Ornithomimids
EXTINCT

Maniraptors

Thyreophorans
EXTINCT

Euornithopods
EXTINCT

Marginocephalians
EXTINCT

RELATIVELY
LONG ARMS
COELUROSAURS

UNEVEN
COVERING
OF ENAMEL
ON TEETH
CERAPODS

3-FINGERED HAND
TETANURANS

INSET
TOOTH ROWS
FORM CHEEKS
GENASAURS

3-TOED FOOT
THEROPODS

GRASPING HAND
SAURISCHIANS

BACKWARD-POINTING
EXTENSION
OF PUBIS BONE
ORNITHISCHIANS

HOLE IN HIP SOCKET
DINOSAURS

ANTORBITAL OPENINGS
ARCHOSAURS

PALATAL OPENINGS
SAUROPSIDS

WATERTIGHT EGG
AMNIOTES

4 LIMBS
TETRAPODS

JAWS
GNATHOSTOMES

VERTEBRAL COLUMN AND BRAINCASE
VERTEBRATES

Halls of MAMMALS and their Extinct Relatives

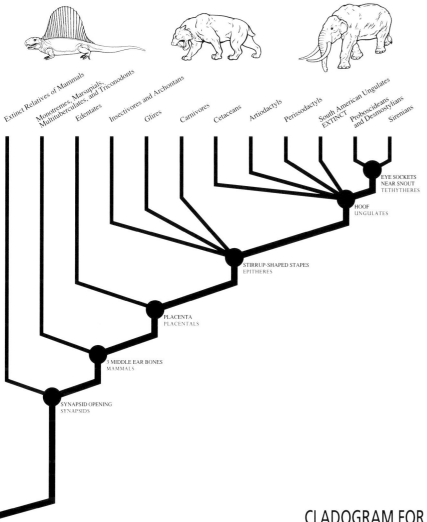

EYE SOCKETS
NEAR SNOUT
TETHYTHERES

HOOF
UNGULATES

STIRRUP-SHAPED STAPES
EPITHERES

PLACENTA
PLACENTALS

3 MIDDLE EAR BONES
MAMMALS

SYNAPSID OPENING
SYNAPSIDS

Extinct Relatives of Mammals

Monotremes, Marsupials,
Multituberculates, and Triconodonts

Edentates

Insectivores and Archontans

Glires

Carnivores

Cetaceans

Artiodactyls

Perissodactyls

South American Ungulates
EXTINCT

Proboscideans
and Desmostylians

Sirenians

CLADOGRAM FOR MAJOR GROUPS IN THE HALLS OF VERTEBRATE EVOLUTION

The animals in The Halls of Vertebrate Evolution are arranged according to their evolutionary relationships. Just as we can trace our family history using a family tree, we can use a similar method to reconstruct evolutionary trees that depict relationships among animals. Each animal is placed on the evolutionary tree with its closest relatives by noting shared features that they inherited from their common ancestor. The main path through the halls represents the trunk of the evolutionary tree. Branching points on the main path represent newly evolved features in the common ancestor that were inherited by animals found on branches originating at that point. Branches off the main path lead into alcoves containing major groups of closely related animals, such as turtles, giant carnivorous dinosaurs, or elephants.

CRETACEOUS PERIOD

Top: This depiction of a scene from the Judith River Formation in southwestern Alberta, Canada, 75 million years ago, shows species such as Euoplocephalus,

CRETACEOUS PERIOD

Middle: Extraordinary animals, like Oviraptor *(right) and* Protoceratops *(left), lived in Mongolia 72 million years ago.*

EOCENE EPOCH

Bottom: Orohippus, *a tiny primitive horse, lived 50 million years ago in southwestern Wyoming.*

OLIGOCENE EPOCH

Top: This group of mammals, in a scene representing southwestern South Dakota 32 million years ago, includes Hoplophoneus (foreground), *a catlike carnivore, and* Mesohippus, *a dog-sized horse.*

MIOCENE EPOCH

Middle: Ten million years ago in southern South Dakota, animals such as Teleoceras (right), *a relative of the modern rhinoceros, and* Neohipparion (left), *an extinct horse, roamed the plains.*

PLEISTOCENE EPOCH

Bottom: Smilodon, *a saber-toothed cat, stalks prey in this scene from the Los Angeles Basin of 30,000 years ago.*

of noises *Barosaurus* made—a low roar, a subtle hiss, or nothing at all. And finally we would reiterate the point made downstairs that the fossils do not tell us with any certainty whether the animal, in fact, could rear up, although such actions may have been important for feeding in the treetops or defending its young.

Fossils like those of the *Barosaurus* tell us many startling facts about the history of life on Earth, but they do not reveal all of life's past secrets. As visitors walk through the exhibition halls, the labels will help them understand what is known and not known about our long-lost evolutionary cousins.

After visitors pass the barosaur, they are introduced to

The black path on the floor represents the trunk of the vertebrate evolutionary tree and leads visitors through displays of major adaptations in vertebrate evolution.

the two main lines of evidence that can be followed through evolutionary history. Along one side of the hall, a set of chronologically ordered murals, which form the basis for one of the primary interactive computer systems that appear throughout the halls, introduces people to the expanse of geologic time and vertebrate evolution. Globes accompanying the murals illustrate the changing positions of the continents at various periods in the past. Twelve scenes are depicted, ranging in age and environment from a marine scene about 360 million years old that explores the origin of vertebrates to a terrestrial scene only 12,000 years old that focuses on the large mammalian fauna at the end of the last Ice Age. The computer program, called Timelines, allows visitors to choose a past period in evolutionary history to which they would like to return. Once a choice is made, the map of the Earth on the screen transforms as the continents move back into the positions that they occupied at the

time chosen. Cross-hairs pinpoint the position of the place on the globe to which the visitor will travel, and an image of the environment at that location appears on the screen. From there, the visitor is free to roam around the scene, learning about the environments and the ancient animals that lived in them.

Another large wall that forms the other side of the hall supports an enormous family tree for vertebrates. It is used to explain how the evolutionary pathway that runs throughout the exhibition halls works, and a navigational guide is provided so that visitors can quickly discern where to find their favorite specimens.

The primary structure of the exhibition is different from that in most exhibits about evolutionary history. Whereas most presentations emphasize the chronologically ordered walk through time, these halls are structured to reflect the evolutionary relationships among vertebrates, more specifically, our human relationship to other vertebrates.

The concept is simple; the goal is to reconstruct the sequence of vertebrate evolution through a method of grouping animals called cladistics. Here's how it works.

Although at first glance the diversity of life seems overwhelming, we see a pattern in that diversity when we search for anatomical characteristics that are shared by different organisms. This pattern of features can be used to arrange organisms into smaller groups contained within larger groups. For example, some features are shared by a large number of organisms. Fish, frogs, lizards, and humans all have a head and a backbone composed of small individual bones called vertebrae and are thus all included in a large group called vertebrates. Vertebrates inherited their head and backbone from the very first vertebrate or, in other words, the common ancestor. We may not have found fossils of this common ancestor because the fossil record is not complete, but we argue that because of the widespread presence of heads and backbones among vertebrates, these features were present in the common ancestor. Therefore the group called vertebrates contains all the descendants of this ancestor.

Other features are shared by a smaller group of animals within vertebrates. For instance, frogs, lizards, and humans all have four limbs, with bony wrists, ankles, fingers, and toes. These animals belong to a group called tetrapods (meaning "four-footed"), and they descended from the first animal with distinct wrists, ankles, fingers, and toes.

Finally, lizards and humans both develop from eggs that contain a watertight membrane, called the amnion, which surrounds the growing embryo and prevents it from drying out. These representatives of the reptilian and mammalian lineages, respectively, belong to a group within tetrapods called amniotes, named for the watertight membrane, and they descended from the first animal in which the amnion evolved.

Consequently, this arrangement of groups within groups is interpreted to reflect the sequence of evolution as descendants inherit new or advanced features from their ancestors. By following the sequence from larger groups into smaller groups, we can follow the order in which newly advanced features arose. Because having a head and backbone is more widespread among vertebrates than having four limbs, the head and backbone are thought to have evolved first. The fossil record appears to confirm this sequence since the earliest-known vertebrate lived about 500 million years ago, whereas the first-known tetrapod dates back only about 350 million years. Similarly, the evolution of four limbs is thought to have preceded the evolution of the watertight amnion because the distribution of four limbs is more widespread within tetrapods than the distribution of the amnion. Accordingly, the earliest-known amniote arose about 50 million years after the first-known tetrapod.

But how can we best depict this approach for reconstructing evolutionary history? People trace their family history by compiling a family tree. In a somewhat similar way, scientists depict evolutionary history by compiling evolutionary trees that show close and distant relatives. In our exhibition, branching diagrams, called cladograms, represent the evolutionary tree for vertebrates and are used to show the sequence of evolution. A branching point on the tree represents the evolution of the advanced feature that characterizes a group of animals occupying the branches that originate from that point. By starting at the bottom of the tree and reading up branching point by branching point, we can reconstruct the order, discussed above, in which new features arose.

Walking along the black main path through the fossil halls is like walking along the trunk of the vertebrate evolutionary tree. There are circular branching points along the main path that represent the evolution of new or advanced features, such as backbones, four limbs, and the watertight amnion. At each branching point, you can walk off the main path or trunk of the tree to explore alcoves, which represent the branches of the tree and contain a group of closely related animals, such as sharks or duckbill dinosaurs. Each alcove contains an information station where you can find out general information about the group and use the interactive Lifelines computer programs to learn from the museum's curators about the advanced features that evolved within that group.

One advantage of arranging the specimens as if you are walking along an evolutionary tree is that you see various sharks or dinosaurs in one area of the exhibit, making it easier to follow the course of evolution by comparing primitive and advanced members within the group.

The view of evolutionary history seen in these halls represents the best interpretation of the available scientific evidence according to the curators at the American Museum of Natural History. These views, like all scientific ideas, are continually subject to change and refinement. Further research and the discovery of new fossils may well modify our present understanding.

The two lines of evidence, the Timelines murals and the vertebrate evolutionary tree, lead visitors into a large theater, where a video presentation integrates these two lines of evolutionary evidence by outlining the major events in the history of animals with backbones, focusing especially on the major episodes of radiations and extinctions that have altered the course of vertebrate evolution. The first part of the video leads up to the origin of vertebrates.

Vertebrate life is amazingly diverse. Vertebrates are tiny, and they are enormous. They walk on land and swim in the ocean. They burrow underground, and they fly through the air. Vertebrates live in the coldest places on earth and in the hottest. They eat plants; they eat meat; and they eat insects. They are solitary, and they are social. And lest we forget, we humans are vertebrates.

In view of this stunning array of diversity, what makes a vertebrate a vertebrate? A common definition is that vertebrates have a bony backbone. Except for a few vertebrates that have a backbone made of material more like cartilage, this view is correct. But paleontologists are interested in the evolutionary history of vertebrates; we try to figure out where it all began. The vertebrates we look for lived millions, and even hundreds of millions, of years ago.

When ancient vertebrates died, their soft parts, like skin and organs, rotted away. All that usually remains are the harder parts of the body, such as bones and teeth. Much of the original organic material in these elements is replaced by minerals that precipitate from the ground water that seeps through the sediments in which the carcass was buried so that the elements are preserved as fossils. Only a very small sample of all the vertebrates that have lived over the last 500 million years are preserved as fossils. In other words, as Darwin noted in the nineteenth century, the fossil record is very incomplete.

The fossils that we do find represent the ultimate antiques of evolutionary history. They provide us with glimpses of a far distant past, and they are the key to reconstructing the fascinating evolutionary history of vertebrate life on Earth, a story that begins 3.5 billion years ago, with the first strand of DNA. With the evolution of this basic component, life originated. From there, paleontologists use an evolutionary tree of life to show both the sequence of evolution of new anatomical features and kinship relationships among organisms.

The next branching point further up on the cladogram represents the evolution of cells that have a nucleus inside to house the DNA. The earliest fossil evidence for this feature is found in rocks between 1.5 and 2.0 billion years old. These organisms form a group called eukaryotes, which basically means "true nucleus." At this point, plants branch off on the tree to establish their own evolutionary lineage, but our journey toward the origin of vertebrates continues on to the branches for animals.

About 700 million years ago, the first animal evolved with cells arranged in discrete layers. All these animals belong to a group called metazoans.

Vertebrate history begins about 500 million years ago. With these animals comes the evolution of a head, braincase, and the first step in the evolution of a backbone. All the animals that occur on branches of the tree that originate at this point, including fish, amphibians, reptiles, birds, and mammals, share this essential feature. The head serves as a center for coordinating sensory input and the backbone provides support for the muscles that helped early vertebrates swim through their aquatic environment in search of food.

The video continues on to discuss other major events in the evolution of vertebrates, developments that we will encounter in the later chapters that feature the different groups of vertebrates.

3 BUILDING THE VERTEBRATE BODY:

This view of the Hall of Vertebrate Origins shows the specimens hanging from the ornate ceiling over the main evolutionary path. Fossils include jaws from an extinct great white shark (Carcharodon), a large Cretaceous marine fish (Xiphactinus), a long-necked plesiosaur (Thallasomedon), a giant turtle (Stupendemys), and two pteosaurs (Pteranodon and Tupuxuara).

THE HALL OF VERTEBRATE ORIGINS

VERTEBRATES: THE MAJOR GROUPS AND THEIR EVOLUTIONARY RELATIONSHIPS

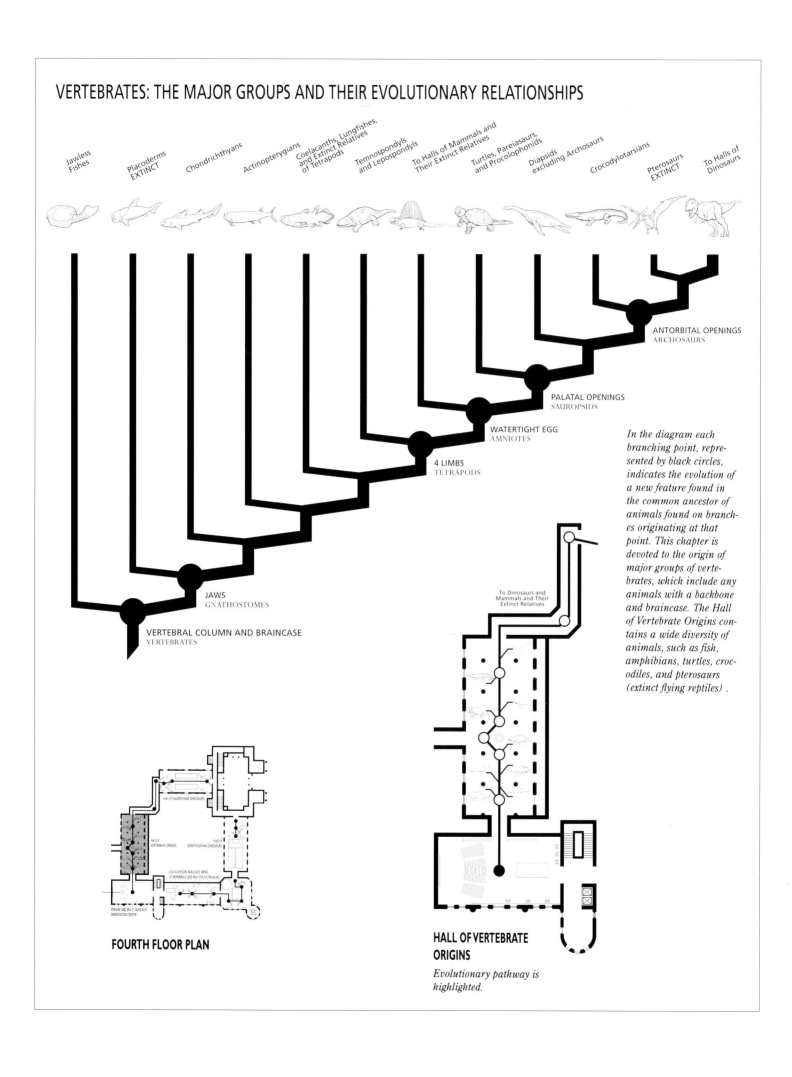

Jawless Fishes

Placoderms
EXTINCT

Chondrichthyans

Actinopterygians

Coelacanths, Lungfishes, and Extinct Relatives of Tetrapods

Temnospondyls and Lepospondyls

To Halls of Mammals and Their Extinct Relatives

Turtles, Pareiasaurs, and Procolophonids

Diapsids excluding Archosaurs

Crocodylotarsians

Pterosaurs
EXTINCT

To Halls of Dinosaurs

ANTORBITAL OPENINGS
ARCHOSAURS

PALATAL OPENINGS
SAUROPSIDS

WATERTIGHT EGG
AMNIOTES

4 LIMBS
TETRAPODS

JAWS
GNATHOSTOMES

VERTEBRAL COLUMN AND BRAINCASE
VERTEBRATES

In the diagram each branching point, represented by black circles, indicates the evolution of a new feature found in the common ancestor of animals found on branches originating at that point. This chapter is devoted to the origin of major groups of vertebrates, which include any animals with a backbone and braincase. The Hall of Vertebrate Origins contains a wide diversity of animals, such as fish, amphibians, turtles, crocodiles, and pterosaurs (extinct flying reptiles).

To Dinosaurs and Mammals and Their Extinct Relatives

FOURTH FLOOR PLAN

HALL OF VERTEBRATE ORIGINS

Evolutionary pathway is highlighted.

Upon leaving the Orientation Center and entering the Hall of Vertebrate Origins, visitors will be struck immediately by the classic grandeur of this venerable exhibition space with its ornate columns and arches. The exhibition designers were especially insistent that we celebrate not only our evolutionary history but also our architectural heritage. It was clear from our first adventures of climbing up into the attic above the hung ceiling of acoustical tile in this hall that by exposing these original architectural elements, we would again be able to set our exhibition apart from the presentations of evolutionary history in other museums.

The trend in most contemporary exhibitions is to construct them inside a "black box." In essence, this means that all the natural light entering through the windows must be blacked out. The advantage is that this allows the designer to create a more dramatic environment. Blocking out the natural light can create darkened areas where a spectacular specimen can be exquisitely and theatrically lit. By controlling the light and using artificial lighting visitors can be "surprised" when they walk around a partition into a space dominated by an impressive special effect, like a robotic dinosaur. This strategy is in stark contrast to the way exhibits used to be done.

Photos from our archives illustrate that before the advent of electricity, the problems of exhibit designers did not involve how to keep natural light out but rather how to get enough light in. This was particularly true in this first building of the museum designed by Calvert Vaux. It housed part of the library immediately before we began this renovation project. After its completion in 1877 at a cost of $700,000 the fourth floor of this building was furnished with exhibit cases containing the original geological exhibits in the museum. Even in its early days, however, vertebrate fossils began to sneak in among the columns. In 1887 the museum acquired a mastodon skeleton and placed it on exhibition in this building. Nonetheless, the space played the role of a Geology Hall until the middle of the second decade of the twentieth century, when it was transformed into a hall that contained invertebrate fossils as well as mineral specimens. Not until 1961 was the library moved into this space.

Vaux's design for the geology exhibition hall called for a series of narrow slitlike windows to be situated between larger gracefully arched window frames. When I first saw these narrow windows, I had trouble imagining what they were for; they reminded me of slits in fortifications through which soldiers fired their weapons. But after looking at the archival photos, their function became very apparent. An exhibit case had extended out from each of these slits toward the midline of the hall, and each window had actually occupied a position on the side of the case so that natural light coming through the window illuminated the specimens inside.

Our fossil mounts, many of which are large, will have no trouble holding their own in these expansive spaces bathed in natural light. Along one side of this hall, the external facade has been restored and left uncluttered so that visitors can appreciate how the outside of the first building originally looked.

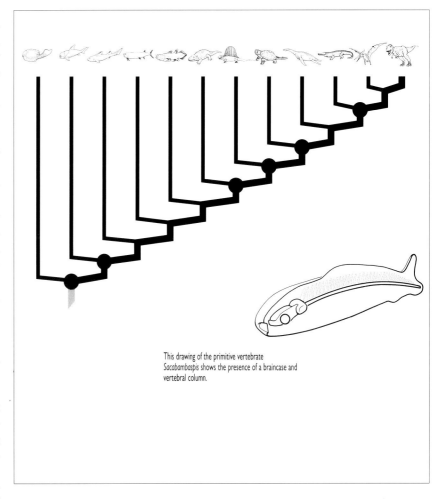

This drawing of the primitive vertebrate *Sacabambaspis* shows the presence of a braincase and vertebral column.

This is the branching point for all vertebrates. All vertebrates share the common features of a braincase and a vertebral column, which they inherited from their common ancestor, the first vertebrate. Vertebrates include fish, amphibians, reptiles, dinosaurs (including birds), and mammals.

Stupendemys, *a
gigantic turtle with a
shell about 8 feet in
length, hangs suspended
near restored columns
in the new Hall of
Vertebrate Origins.*

As was described in the last chapter, a walk through The Halls of Vertebrate Evolution resembles a walk along the trunk and branches of an evolutionary tree. The branching points along the trunk of the tree represent the evolution of a new characteristic that is shared by all the animals on the branches further along. Most of the important evolutionary adaptations that form the basic building blocks of the vertebrate body will be featured in this first hall.

The story begins with the initial stages in the evolution of the primary support structure for which vertebrates are named, the backbone. This line of vertebrae situated along the midline of the back provides attachment points for the myriad of muscles that vertebrates use for locomotion. Vertebrates swim through the water by using the segmented muscles attached to their vertebral column to generate wavelike undulations. These undulations, easily recognizable in the movements of most living fish, push the body against the water to generate a forward thrust. The backbone also helps make these movements more energy efficient by preventing the body from shortening as the muscles contract.

Actually, the earliest vertebrates did not have a bony backbone. However, some had a segmented series of spines that ran along the back which may well represent the first step in the evolution of a backbone. Only later in evolutionary history did bony backbones appear. Nonetheless, bone embedded in the skin and a well-developed head were present in the earliest vertebrates. Bone served the function of providing the body with a protective covering of durable armor. It is a kind of tissue found only in vertebrates. Other kinds of bony tissue, all of which are formed primarily by crystals of the mineral called apatite, include the enamel on teeth and the bones of the internal skeleton that form first in cartilage before transforming into bone. Our earliest vertebrate kin extracted life-supporting oxygen from the water through gills, as do living fish, rather than through the lungs. The head in these earliest vertebrates featured a chambered brain and several sensory receiving devices that we take for granted, including a nose, paired eyes, and ears. These organs generated a significantly enhanced ability to monitor conditions and events within the aquatic environment. In reality, it was these changes associated with the development of a more sophisticated brain and head that constituted the most profound evolutionary changes surrounding the origin of vertebrates.

Examples of the earliest-known vertebrates, almost 500 million years old, can be found in the group of jawless fish called ostracoderms. These animals, such as *Sacabambaspis* from South America, ranged from only a couple of inches to almost one foot in length and possessed a head that was protected both on the top and bottom by bony plates. The mouth was also surrounded by small bony plates; however, no jaws were present. In some, the eyes were placed far apart on the skull. The rest of the body and the tail were covered by large overlapping scales. There is no trace of a bony backbone or a bony internal skeleton. Because of the absence of paired fins in the shoulder and pelvic regions of most ostracoderms, as well as the absence of a dorsal fin on top of the back, these animals were proba-

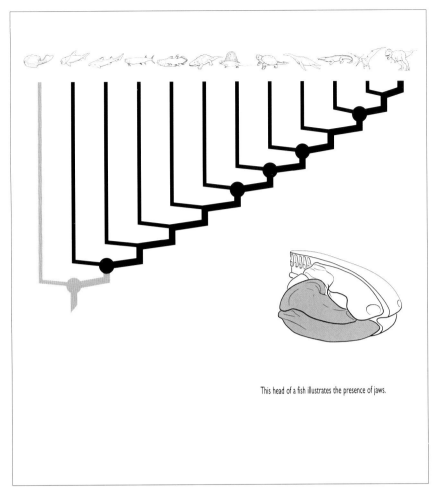

This head of a fish illustrates the presence of jaws.

This is the branching point for gnathostomes, vertebrates with jaws. Jaws evolved in the common ancestor of gnathostomes. They provide an anchorage for the powerful muscles and a support for the teeth that are important in feeding for most vertebrates.

Dunkleosteus

Bothriolepis

bly not accomplished swimmers. The most primitive living vertebrates are the hagfish and lamprey—long, slender, jawless, parasitic fish that have no bones or scales.

The next step along the trunk of the evolutionary tree leads toward an evolutionary innovation that changed the way most vertebrates feed, including our own species. The earliest-known vertebrates basically sucked food in through the jawless mouth. It is unlikely that they were skilled predators. In contrast, the evolution of jaws provided a powerfully mobile structure for biting as a way of capturing or gathering and eating food. In jawed vertebrates, or gnathostomes, the upper and lower jaws are hinged together and attached to strong muscles that are used to close the mouth. The evolution of these unique and usually bony mouth parts represented an important adaptation which enhanced the predatory abilities of most vertebrates and provided them with the opportunity to exploit a vast variety of new food sources, including other vertebrates.

One limb of the evolutionary tree originating from this branching point leads to the first group of jawed vertebrates to dominate the oceans. These heavily armored fish are called placoderms, and they proliferated about 410 million years ago before becoming extinct about 365 million years ago. The global diversity they generated within this 45-million-year span is astounding, as documented by the presence of both large and small forms and presumed habitats that ranged from bottom dwellers to active, open-ocean predators.

The most intimidating placoderms evolved within a group called arthrodires, which possessed a pair of self-sharpening bones that formed the upper and lower jaws. These were equipped with serrated cutting edges and a sharp bony cusp at the front. Some arthrodires, such as *Dunkleosteus,* may have reached lengths up to sixteen feet, but the business end of this predator was centered in the massively armored head. None of the sharks or bony fishes that lived at the same time evolved bodies of similar size.

Another even more bizarre group of placoderms contains the antiarchs. In their ungainly appearance they resembled aquatic tanks: most of the body was covered by bony plates, and the head was contained within a rounded head shield. Instead of fins, antiarchs had armored, jointed appendages that were built somewhat like crabs' legs. Fossils of antiarchs have been found on almost every continent, documenting their widespread geographic distribution.

A more commonly recognized group that branched off the tree at the point where jaws evolved is the one that includes sharks, rays, skates, and rabbitfishes—the chondrichthyans. Predominantly represented by predators and scavengers, the earliest-known members of the group arose over 360 million years ago, and they have inhabited both fresh- and salt water environments.

Sharks and their kin arose from a common ancestor that had an internal skeleton made of cartilage that has a layer of calcium phosphate prisms situated near the surface. This is the same basic kind of material that makes up bone, but none of the shark skeleton is made up of solid bone. Complete fossil skeletons, therefore, are almost unknown.

Nonetheless, the fossil record for sharks is fairly complete as a result of their durable, enamel-coated teeth.

Shark teeth are among the most common of vertebrate fossils, facilitated in large part by the evolution of a system of rapid tooth replacement that operates throughout the animal's life, producing as many as twelve to fifteen thousand individual teeth in one lifetime. The teeth are arranged in rows that form next to the tongue and are carried out toward the lip, as if they were on a conveyor belt. This motion is generated by the movement of gum tissues to which the teeth are attached. In turn, the teeth are attached to the cartilaginous jaws and the gum tissue by fibers. When they reach a position next to the lip, they are worn and fall out. The edges of the teeth are often serrated like a steak knife or sculpted into sharp pointed cusps. The shapes differ in different kinds of sharks, as well as according to age, position in the mouth, and even sex. In contrast to sharks, rays have teeth with flattened surfaces that fit together like a mosaic to form bony plates in the upper and lower jaws. Many rays use these plates to crush the shells of invertebrate prey.

Modern sharks total about 250 species, whereas rays and their kin total more than 350 species, but there is little doubt about which animal within the group ranks as the most fearsome of all time. That distinction goes to an extinct relative of the living great white shark. This beast, known as *Carcharodon megalodon,* lived roughly 12 to 15 million years ago in marine environments and reached a length of forty feet. This is just an estimate because, in actuality, no complete skeleton is known—just a few large circular vertebrae and, more commonly, teeth. (As a comparison, remember that living great white sharks may reach about twenty feet in length.) Some of the serrated, triangular teeth in the fossil great white are as much as six inches long, and the jaws themselves could open to a height of five feet.

Slightly farther down the trunk of the evolutionary tree, visitors encounter the alcove devoted to the largest group of modern vertebrates—the ray-finned fish. These include most of the commonly recognized fish in the world, such as trout, tuna, bass, salmon, perch, barracuda, sardines, mackerel, sturgeons, gars, etc. In fact, there are over 20,000 living species of ray-finned fish. The group is named for the fins that contain a fanlike array of soft or spiny struts attached to a few small bones at the base of the fin. The scientific name for this group is actinopterygians, and the earliest representatives date from around 400 million years ago.

Most of the diversity within ray-finned fish is contained within a subgroup called teleosts. In addition to tuna, trout, salmon, and other common food fish, this group includes such odd forms as eels and seahorses. The more typical teleosts exhibit improved buoyancy, a light but bony skeleton, and a tail fin that generates more efficient propulsion for swimming. An additional adaptation related to feeding involves the evolution of movable bones in the jaws. As a result, the mouth expands laterally when it opens, which serves to suck food into the mouth and facilitates the capture of larger prey.

This area of the hall is dominated by two fossils of a giant ray-finned fish called *Xiphactinus,* which lived about 70 to 80 million years ago in a shallow continental seaway that

Xiphactinus *was an intimidating, late Cretaceous marine predator with massive, heavily toothed jaws.*

Drepanaspis, *an*
example of a placoderm,
roamed the seas until
about 365 million
years ago.

Some arthrodires, such as
the 360-million-year-old
predator Dunkleosteus,
may have reached lengths
of 16 feet.

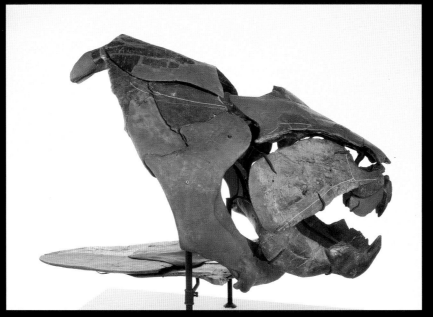

Facing page:
Some fossil fish from the
110-million-year-old
Santana Formation of
Brazil are found to
contain the remains of
their last meal.

Lungfish such as this
specimen of
Scaumenacia, *a 360-*
million-year-old, lobe-
finned fish, used their
lungs for breathing, but
also their gills.

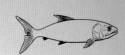

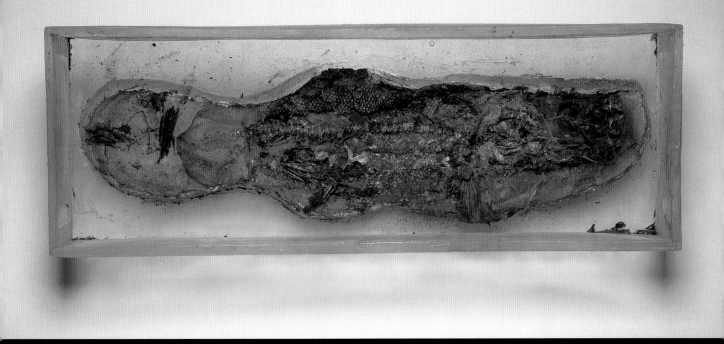

covered what is now Kansas. It shared this seaway with marine reptiles including the long-necked plesiosaurs and titanic marine lizards called mosasaurs. *Xiphactinus* was apparently an intimidating predator that propelled itself with a powerful tail and captured prey using its massive and heavily toothed jaws. As the three-dimensional cast and two-dimensional skeletal plaque illustrate, adults reach lengths of more than twenty feet.

One can speculate about what some of these ancient vertebrates ate based on the shape of their teeth, but in reality, these are usually just guesses. To be sure about an extinct animal's diet, the food must be preserved inside the ribcage of the fossil skeleton. Only in very rare circumstances has such dietary evidence been documented. One set of such occurrences has been recovered from a series of 110-million-year-old fossil fish found in Brazil. The curator of fossil fish at the museum, John Maisey, has examined hundreds of specimens in an attempt to interpret parts of the food chain that existed within this ancient community. Because these fossils were preserved in hard limestone, the specimens are not prepared in the usual way, using sharp needles, dental picks, and miniature sand blasters. Instead, they are immersed in weak acid, which, if done carefully by a skilled preparator, dissolves the limestone without damaging the fossil bone. If successful, what remains is a delicate, three-dimensional skeleton of a long-extinct animal packed with scientifically valuable information.

Evidence that Maisey used to reconstruct the food pyramid within the ancient sea that covered the part of Brazil where the fossil fish were found includes a number of juvenile specimens of the fish *Rhacolepis.* Many were found with small shrimps preserved in their stomach. In some specimens, the stomach wall can be seen enveloping the shrimp. Older individuals of the same genus appeared to have preferred a diet of small fishes. *Rhacolepis* was, in turn, eaten by larger predatory fish, such as *Cladocyclus,* which in at least one case apparently swallowed the *Rhacolepis* whole. Farther up the food pyramid, *Cladocyclus* comprised a favorite meal of top predators, such as *Calamopleurus.* Even to a paleontologist, it seems quite remarkable to be able to peer under the water of a sea more than 100 million years old and spy on the feeding habits of the local denizens.

On the next branch of the evolutionary tree, we encounter the groups of fish most closely related to us and other four-limbed vertebrates, lungfish, coelacanths, and an extinct group called osteolepiforms. The common name for these groups is "lobe-finned" fish because the bones at the base of the fin are supported by large muscles that form a fleshy lobe. All these groups arose from a common ancestor with paired fins in which a single bone fits up against the shoulder or pelvis. Since our arms and legs are built in the same way, we are also members of this group called sarcopterygians.

Until recently, coelacanths were one of the most mysterious groups of fish. They appeared in the fossil record about 380 million years ago, and over the course of their evolutionary history they inhabited both fresh-water and marine environments. Freshwater coelacanths apparently disappeared when an estuary formed about 110 million years ago

Notelops

Scaumenacia

as South America drifted away from Africa, but marine forms lived in shallow continental seas until about 65 million years ago. No fossils are known from younger rocks at all, so paleontologists long assumed that the group became extinct at about the same time that the large dinosaurs did on land. But in 1938 that changed when a living coelacanth was caught in deep marine waters off Madagascar. Extant coelacanths live along the steep volcanic slopes of the Comoro Islands, where they spend much of their time curiously swimming upside down.

The earliest-known lungfishes appeared about 400 million years ago, and there are still three living genera distributed across the southern hemisphere. They live in shallow, fresh-water environments, where they use their strong jaws and sturdy tooth plates to crush the shells of their invertebrate prey or grind up vegetation. All three living forms utilize their lungs for breathing, but they also have gills; the degree to which they breathe oxygen through their lungs varies widely. In fact, it is assumed that most primitive bony fish had lungs.

There are some extinct sarcopterygian fishes called osteolepiforms that are among our closest "fishy" relatives. These fossil forms, such as *Eusthenopteron,* have been studied extensively by paleontologists because they share advanced features with primitive tetrapods. One such feature is an internal nostril within the roof of the mouth. *Eusthenopteron* lived alongside early lungfish in what is now part of Quebec about 375 million years ago.

Just a few steps farther down the trunk of our evolutionary tree takes visitors across a momentous threshold in our history—the evolution of limbs with distinct wrists, ankles, fingers, and toes. In the earliest members of this group, the basic arrangement of bones in the front and hind limbs is actually very similar to ours. In addition to having a single bone that fits up against the shoulder in the front limb and the hip in the rear limb, two slightly thinner bones in both the front and hind limbs form the next section leading away from the body. These provide the limbs with a greater range of maneuverability. Finally, farthest from the body, the complex of bones forming the wrists, ankles, fingers, and toes is arranged in a way to create flexibility for locomotion.

Animals with four well-developed limbs are called tetrapods, which appropriately means "four-footed"; it is important to note, however, that through the process of evolution, the limbs of tetrapods have become adapted for an astounding number of activities besides simply supporting the body on land. In terms of locomotion, they represent the main structures responsible for running in horses, jumping in frogs, flying in birds, climbing in koalas, digging in moles, and swimming in seals. Besides locomotion, limbs are often essential for capturing prey, gathering vegetation, and even writing books like this.

Clearly, the evolution of limbs at this branching point eventually catalyzed our ancestral transition to life on land. Many of the features important for life on land did not just appear suddenly, but evolved, at least in rudimentary forms, earlier in some of our aquatic ancestors. We have already noted that sturdy fins with single bones attaching to the shoulder and hip evolved in lungfish and their relatives about 400 million years ago; rudimentary lungs were also present in these same fish. It is becoming increasingly clear that these features were originally related to life in the water rather than life on land. Consequently, the old idea that the first animals to evolve limbs did so in order to leave the water to pursue prey on land is not consistent with the fossil record.

Accordingly, recent discoveries have suggested that the earliest-known tetrapods, such as *Acanthostega* (a model of which has been elegantly sculpted by Eliot Goldfinger), were primarily adapted for living in water. We should note, for example, their full set of gills for extracting oxygen from water and their complete, well-developed tail fin. In actuality, early tetrapods probably used these features, as well as their limbs, for swimming and maneuvering through the water rather than for terrestrial locomotion. Only later did tetrapods exploit their limbs to colonize the continents.

There are two groups of primitive tetrapods. The lepospondyls contain a number of rather unusual and grotesque forms that are all now extinct, whereas the temnospondyls include the first large amphibious tetrapods, as well as the living amphibians such as frogs and salamanders.

Although lepospondyls include some extinct animals that superficially resemble lizards and snakes, many early evolutionary experiments within this group tended toward the bizarre—*Diplocaulus,* for example. It was apparently aquatic, an inference based partially on the fact that its fossils are found in sediments that were deposited in ancient streams and lakes. Most parts of the skeleton are not particularly noteworthy, including its rather short limbs and the long flattened tail that was apparently used for propelling itself through the water as it swam. When examining a complete fossil skeleton of the animal, however, one's attention is immediately drawn to the disproportionately large, boomerang-shaped skull. Our exhibition displays an exceptionally complete fossilized growth sequence for this animal, which documents how the skull attained its unusual appearance. The winglike bones that form the boomerang clearly grew at a faster rate than the other bones of the skull. The adaptational significance of the skull has been the subject of intense speculation, but its true function remains a mystery, although it must have affected the way the animal swam.

The other group of primitive tetrapods—temnospondyls —include the earliest large amphibious tetrapods, such as *Eryops, Mastodonsaurus,* and *Buettneria.* Although only distantly related, their living relatives include amphibians, such as frogs and salamanders. All these animals arose from a common ancestor that developed from a larval stage and had only four fingers. As shown by evidence in fossil trackways, they were the first major group of vertebrates to live extensively on land and use their limbs primarily for land-based locomotion. Their eggs were not watertight, however, as their larval form of development shows, and they had to return to the water in order to reproduce. The general skeletal form of the earlier representatives is typified by *Eryops,* with its well-developed limbs and large skull with a rounded snout. The relatively small conical teeth arranged around the margin of the mouth are supplemented by impressive tusklike teeth that protruded from

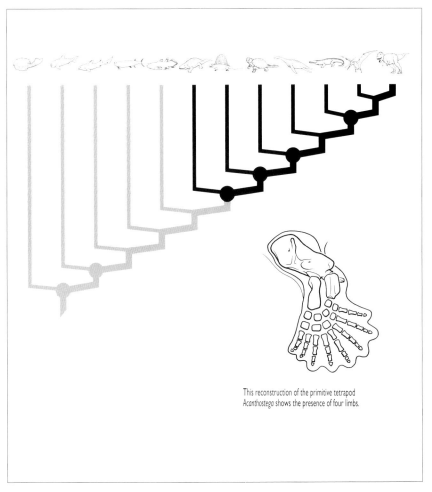

This reconstruction of the primitive tetrapod *Acanthostega* shows the presence of four limbs.

Acanthostega

Diplocaulus

Eryops

Mastodonsaurus

One of the most significant events in vertebrate history was the evolution of four limbs in the common ancestor of tetrapods. Limbs became adapted for a great variety of locomotory modes, including running, jumping, flying, climbing, and swimming. The four limbs of tetrapods allowed later members of the group to move out of the water and onto the land.

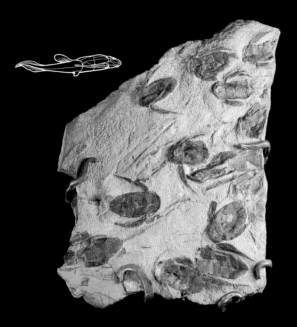

The antiarchs, a group
within placoderms,
contains such animals
as the 360-million-
year-old Bothriolepis,
a kind of swimming,
armored tank.

Acanthostega, *which
lived 360 million years
ago, is one of the
earliest known
tetrapods, animals that
have four limbs with
distinct wrists, ankles,
fingers, and toes.*

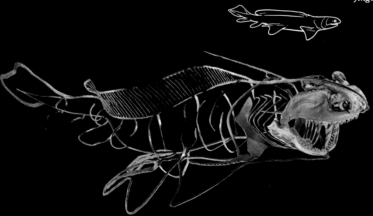

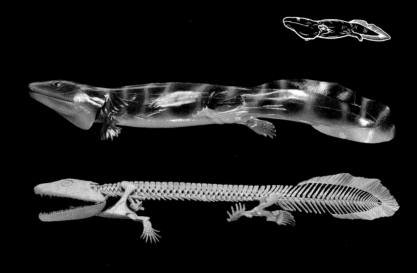

Sharks, *such as the 280-
million year old*
Orthocanthus, *evolved
a system of tooth
replacement that
operates throughout the
animal's life.*

The boomerang-shaped
head of Diplocaulus *may
have affected the way that
this 275-million-year-old
animal swam.*

Large amphibious tetrapods such as Eryops, *which lived 280 million years ago, are distantly related to living frogs and salamanders.*

A 280-million-year-old relative of frogs was Dissorophus. *It had a covering of armor on its back, like that of an armadillo.*

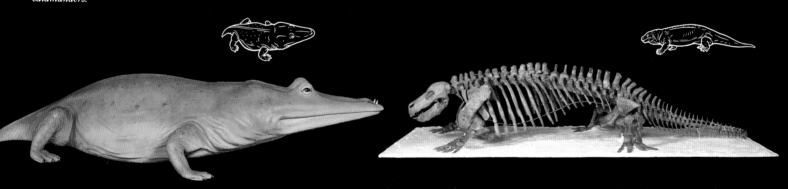

Mastodonsaurus *had tusklike teeth that protruded through the roof of this 250-million-year-old animal's mouth.*

This 280-million-year-old Diadectes *was probably closely related to the ancestor of reptiles and mammals.*

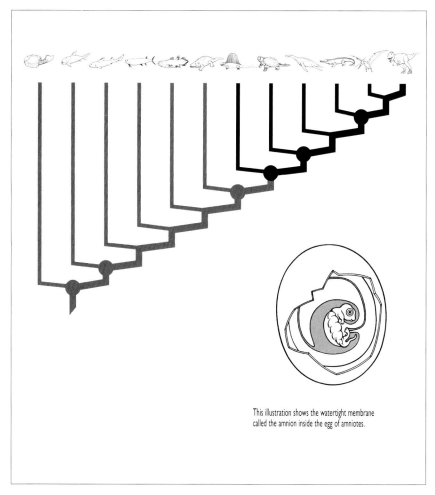

This illustration shows the watertight membrane called the amnion inside the egg of amniotes.

Turtles, lizards, crocodiles, dinosaurs (including birds), and mammals are amniotes. These animals inherited the watertight egg from their common ancestor. A watertight membrane inside the egg prevents the egg from drying out and allows amniotes to lay their eggs on land. They were thus freed from returning to the water to reproduce and could live their entire lives on land.

Dissorophus

Diadectes

the roof of the mouth. This battery of sharp teeth implies that *Eryops* was a predator, perhaps using its palatal tusks to impale its fleshy prey in a way similar to that of the modern crocodile.

The term amphibian means "double life." This makes the name very appropriate for frogs, salamanders, and their relatives since they all go through a larval stage before reaching adulthood. The most common example is the tadpole, which is the larval stage of a frog. Usually, the larva is quite different in shape, habits, and diet from the adult; no one understands, however, exactly what advantage in evolutionary terms a larval stage represents.

The living amphibians arose from a single common ancestor that had a special extension on the squamosal bone in the skull where the eardrum attached. This arrangement may have improved their ability to hear airborne sounds. In addition, the teeth are flexibly attached to the jaws, which may aid in holding prey. Despite the amphibians' need to return to the water to lay eggs, they are extremely successful—there are about 4,300 living species—and they can survive inhospitable environmental conditions by lowering their metabolism and slowing their growth.

Paleontologists have found fossils of an early relative of frogs called *Dissorophus*. This animal probably had a covering of armor along its back similar to that of an armadillo, and it may well have been more terrestrial than other temnospondyls of its time.

Leaving the evolutionary trail that led to modern amphibians, we can once again pick up the path leading toward mammals and reptiles. The path leads through a small group of tetrapods called anthracosaurs. Although these animals had probably not yet evolved the hard-shelled, watertight egg that would be necessary to free tetrapods from returning to the water to reproduce, they do share many skeletal features with early reptiles and relatives of mammals. One animal that was probably closely related to the ancestor of reptiles and mammals was *Diadectes*. Its limbs were well developed and clearly able to support the animal's weight on land; the legs, however, sprawled out to the sides of the body. The teeth had complex chewing surfaces for grinding, suggesting that *Diadectes* may have been a plant-eater.

Just a few more steps down the path bring the visitor to the branching point of the evolutionary tree where the watertight egg evolved. All the animals that descended from the first animal with a watertight egg are called amniotes. The group is named for the watertight membrane, termed the amnion, that surrounds the embryo and keeps it from drying out. This is probably the key evolutionary innovation that allowed tetrapods to permanently leave aquatic environments and colonize the land. Within amniotes there are two main branches on the evolutionary tree. One leads to the reptiles (also called sauropsids), such as turtles, lizards, snakes, crocodiles, birds, and a host of extinct relatives including most dinosaurs. The other leads to mammals and their extinct relatives. The last two halls in the loop of six halls are devoted to the evolutionary path leading to our mammalian relatives, but for now we will follow the branch leading toward the reptiles.

The feature that reptiles inherited from their common ancestor was a pair of holes in the roof of the mouth below the eye sockets. In living reptiles, blood vessels and nerves go through these openings, but other than that, the adaptational significance of this evolutionary innovation is not well understood. Perhaps these openings served to lighten the weight of the skull.

At the approximate boundary between the end of the Paleozoic Era and the beginning of the Mesozoic Era, between about 300 million and 250 million years ago, paleontologists have found fossils of several primitive amniotes that possess the suborbital fenestrae in the roof of the mouth that characterize reptiles. One example is an animal called *Scutosaurus,* which belonged to a group called pareiasaurs. These animals became widespread right before the end of the Paleozoic when the present-day continents had become consolidated into a single super land mass called Pangaea. Fossil remains of pareiasaurs have been found in Africa, Europe, and Asia. The skull of *Scutosaurus* was heavily armored with spikes and bony studs. Although we cannot be sure exactly what function(s) the spikes played, it seems probable that they served primarily for protection. The teeth consisted of simple peglike structures that appear to have been more suitable for eating plants than meat.

The most primitive group of reptiles still alive today, the turtles, are actually quite specialized. The group originated at least 225 million years ago, and over the succeeding periods they have exploited a wide variety of terrestrial and aquatic habitats. Turtles are the true paleontologic love of curator Eugene Gaffney, who considers dinosaurs more a social disease than a scientific discipline because there is so much hype and speculation associated with the research about the group. (If he had his way, there would be two halls of turtles rather than two halls of dinosaurs.)

The feature that most obviously signals turtles' distinct specialization is the shell. It is formed by a mosaic of bony plates that are fused to the ribs and vertebrae. Since turtles are still alive today, it is easy for us to observe them and conclude that the shell primarily plays a role in protecting the animal from potential predators. Unlike any other group of vertebrates, the ribs of turtles lie outside the shoulder and hips rather than inside. This facilitates the turtles' commonly seen capability to draw back the legs into the protective shell. In addition, the shell serves as a place of attachment for limb muscles in some aquatic turtles and for fat storage in some terrestrial turtles.

Our knowledge about vertebrate history continues to change with new discoveries. For instance, paleontologists have recently found fossils of an extremely ancient turtle, called *Paleochersis,* in rocks now exposed in Argentina. This discovery extended the fossil record of turtles in South America back almost 60 million years to about 215 million years ago. The earliest and best-known primitive turtle is *Proganochelys,* an animal whose fossils have been found in deposits of similar age in Germany. Even in these most ancient turtles, the shell is complete. Like pareiasaurs, *Proganochelys* even had an impressive array of spikes and other armor on its neck and legs, as well as a macelike club on the end of its tail. The skull and jaw mechanisms, however, are not nearly as specialized as those of later, more advanced turtles.

The 250-million-year-old skull of Scutosaurus *was heavily armored with spikes and bony studs.*

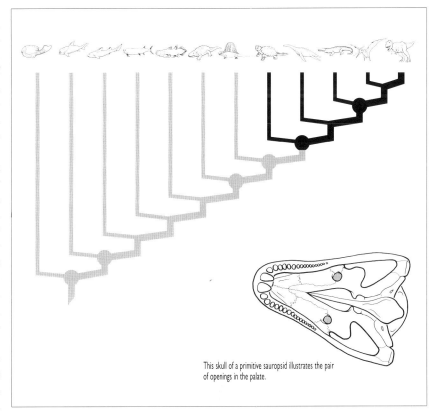

This skull of a primitive sauropsid illustrates the pair of openings in the palate.

Proganochelys

Reptiles or sauropsids, a group that includes turtles, snakes, crocodiles, pterosaurs, and dinosaurs (including birds), inherited a pair of openings in the roof of the mouth from their common ancestor. These openings contain blood vessels and nerves. Animals that existed before the appearance of this newly evolved feature had a mouth with a solid bony roof.

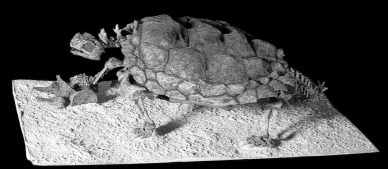

Proganochelys, *an ancient turtle that lived 210 million years ago, is one of the most primitive turtles known.*

A hinged jaw allowed Estesia, a 72-million-year-old, primitive lizard related to living monitors, to open its jaw wide to swallow prey.

The 120,000-year-old Meiolania *was one of the most bizarre turtles. Impressive horns extended back from its skull, and its tail was armed with a bony club.*

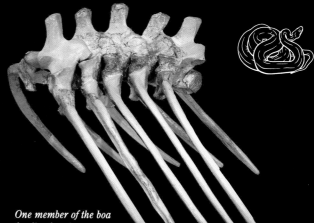

One member of the boa family of snakes, Madstoia, *lived 55 million years ago and reached lengths of 30 feet.*

Rhamphorhynchus
is one of the more
primitive pterosaurs
known. It lived about
140 million years ago
in Europe and had a

Eventually two main groups of turtles evolved, pleurodires and cryptodires. The most obvious difference is found in the way the neck is retracted toward the shell when the animal is threatened. In pleurodires, commonly called the side-necked turtles, the neck bends into a horizontal, S-shaped curve so that it folds under the front edge of the shell. Today pleurodires are limited in their geographic distribution to the continents and oceans of the southern hemisphere, but in earlier times they were more widespread. The largest-known pleurodire was *Stupendemys,* which lived between 5 million and 7 million years ago in what is now Venezuela. This animal may have inhabited freshwater or near-shore marine environments, but we have no clear idea what it included in its diet. Nor do we know why it grew to such enormous size, with a shell approaching eight or nine feet in length.

In contrast to pleurodires, living cryptodires, whose name appropriately means "hidden neck," bend their neck vertically into an S-shaped curve in order to retract it completely inside the shell. In more primitive cryptodires, how-

Thallasomedon

tors encounter a branch for a group of extinct, Mesozoic, marine reptiles—plesiosaurs and ichthyosaurs. Both evolved from as yet undetermined terrestrial reptiles but became readapted for life in the water. Plesiosaurs, which have served as the general model for the mythical monster of Loch Ness, evolved into both short-necked forms, such as *Cryptocleidus,* and long-necked forms, such as the elasmosaurs. In both groups, however, the neck is disproportionately long in relation to that of almost all other vertebrates. At the end of the neck, the jaws of the skull are studded with sharp, conical teeth, presumably for catching fish. Extensive evolutionary modifications of the limb bones reflect changes related to an aquatic lifestyle. The hip and shoulder bones are developed into large, flat sheets to which strong muscles apparently attached which moved the limbs. The limbs themselves were modified into broad flattened flippers or paddles. Short stout bones attached to the shoulder and hip, whereas most of the

Stenopterygius,
a 180-million-year-old ichthyosaur, may have given birth to live young as evidenced by the presence of embryonic bones preserved inside the fossil skeleton of the mother.

ever, the structure of the neck vertebrae suggests that they were not able to retract their neck at all. Today, cryptodires live throughout the world in a wide variety of terrestrial and aquatic environments that range from deserts to the deep oceans. In fact, the only habitats that they are not exploiting are the polar ice caps.

The most bizarre representatives of the cryptodires are the extinct horned turtles, such as the ones belonging to the genus *Meiolania,* which have been found on Lord Howe Island off Australia. These large animals were endowed with impressive bony horns that extended out from the back of the skull, and the tail was armed with a formidable club of bone. Although their fossils have been found in Australia as well as in South America, they were particularly widespread among the volcanic islands of the southern Pacific. Despite this oceanic distribution, they appear to have been predominantly terrestrial and not well suited for swimming distances. It seems probable that they randomly spread from one island to the next as new volcanoes erupted from the sea floor and rose above the ocean's surface, perhaps by floating or riding rafts of debris.

A bit farther along the trunk of the evolutionary tree, visi-

Meiolania

flipper was supported internally by five fingers or toes to which numerous extra bones had been added to increase their length. Plesiosaurs utilized these flippers as the main source of propulsion when they swam, although it is not clear whether they rowed with them, as ducks do with their hind limbs, or whether they flew through the water, as do penguins or sea turtles. The relatively short tail apparently functioned only as a rudder for steering.

In contrast to plesiosaurs, the porpoiselike ichthyosaurs were even more fully evolved for swimming. We have evidence about the form of the body not only from the fossil bones but also because some ichthyosaur fossils preserve the contours of the body outline. Ichthyosaurs were gracefully streamlined from head to tail. The tail itself was developed into a prominent fleshy fin, which served as the main organ for propulsion. The shortened limbs had also evolved into fins for steering that were supported internally by the addition of extra fingers and toes. At the front of the body the skull ended in an elongated snout, and the jaws were armed with dozens of long, sharp teeth. Fossilized stomach contents document that the diet of ichthyosaurs consisted of both fish and squid.

In addition to the host of aquatic adaptations that evolved in ichthyosaurs, one other aspect of their biology was quite unusual for reptiles. All other reptiles, at least so far as we know, reproduced by laying eggs, but some fossils of *Stenopterygius,* document that this advanced ichthyosaur retained the fertilized eggs inside the mother as the embryo developed. Then the mother gave birth to live young. This specimen preserves both the bones of the mother and the embryonic babies inside the mother, suggesting that the mother and babies may have died during the process of birth.

Another branch on the evolutionary tree for reptiles diverges just past the point where ichthyosaurs and plesiosaurs branch off; this branch, however, is populated by reptiles that are much more familiar to us: lizards, snakes, and the lizardlike tuataras or sphenodontids. All these animals belong to a group called lepidosaurs, which arose from a common ancestor that had a uniquely structured ear region that allowed these animals to hear high-frequency sounds through the air. The group's long and rich

tends back into the latest Paleozoic, and even today, lizards are found living on every continent except Antarctica. Most are carnivorous, but some, such as various kinds of iguanas, have evolved into highly specialized herbivores.

Among lizards, the most awesome belong to the group called varanoids: these include monitor lizards, such as the Komodo dragon; extinct Mesozoic, marine lizards, commonly referred to as mosasaurs; and the only poisonous lizards, such as gila monsters and some snakes. All these animals inherited from their common ancestor a hinged lower jaw that allows the mouth to open wider in order to swallow large prey. Monitors, such as the Komodo dragon, are the largest, living, four-legged lizards, reaching lengths of up to ten feet; Komodo dragons, however, would have been dwarfed by the extinct Australian monitor lizard called *Megalania,* which lived at the end of the last Ice Age and reached a length of about twenty feet.

Like their distant relatives, the ichthyosaurs and plesiosaurs, a group of Mesozoic lizards, the mosasaurs, returned to a life in the oceans. Their aquatic adaptations

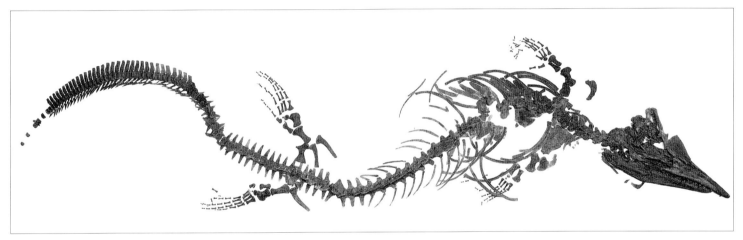

Mosasaurs like Tylosaurus, *which lived 85 million years ago, returned to a life in the sea as evolution transformed limbs into flippers.*

evolutionary history is evident from the number of living species—more than 6,000. Studying the evolution of lizards and snakes is one of the specialties of curator Mark Norell, who also oversaw the development of the Hall of Saurischian Dinosaurs.

Within lepidosaurs, both lizards and snakes belong to another group called squamates, and they inherited a unique nasal structure, called the Jacobson's organ, from their common ancestor. Although you may not be familiar with this organ, you may well be familiar with one aspect of its operation. Snakes characteristically stick their tongue out of the mouth and wave it around. The function of this behavior is to sample chemicals in the air and bring them inside the mouth where they can be analyzed by the Jacobson's organ, which serves in much the same way as our nose does to smell.

Lizards are an extremely diverse group whose members include iguanas, chameleons, geckos, and other advanced lizards, such as *Tupinambis,* gila monsters, monitor lizards, mosasaurs, and snakes. The fossil record of the group ex-

include the modification of limbs into flippers for steering and the development of a long flattened tail for swimming propulsion. One of the largest was the 30-foot-long *Tylosaurus,* which terrorized the ancient shallow seaway that bisected North America from the Gulf of Mexico to the Arctic Ocean at the end of the Mesozoic. Fossilized stomach contents in a few specimens show that this animal's diet consisted of fish and an extinct group of nautiluslike invertebrates called ammonites.

Snakes are the most derived of all squamates and one of the latest groups of reptiles to evolve, first appearing in the fossil record late in the Mesozoic. In essence, snakes are a group of lizards that have "lost" their legs. Perhaps this and other characteristics, such as their poor eyesight and lack of eyelids, reflect the possibility that they arose from a burrowing common ancestor. This is far from certain, and many aspects about the evolutionary origins of snakes remain controversial. What is clear is that snakes are extremely diverse and successful, having adapted to life in habitats that range from the driest deserts to the largest oceans. Living species are found on every continent except Antarctica. The major groups include blind snakes,

Madstoia

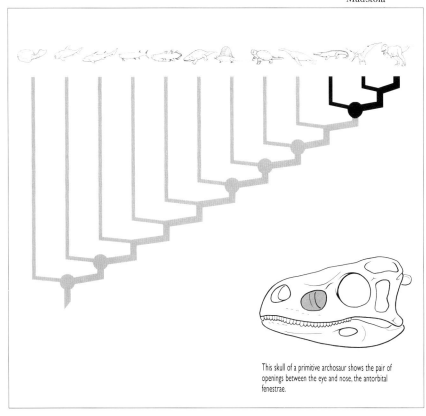

This skull of a primitive archosaur shows the pair of openings between the eye and nose, the antorbital fenestrae.

All archosaurs are descended from a common ancestor that had a pair of openings, known as antorbital fenestrae, between the eye and the nose. Some of the largest and most familiar groups of vertebrates lie within archosaurs, including crocodiles, pterosaurs, and dinosaurs (including birds).

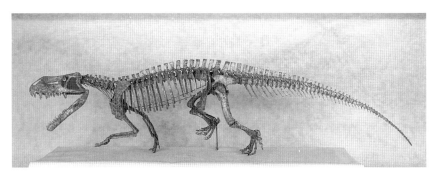

Prestosuchus, *like other archosaurs, has limbs oriented more vertically than more primitive reptiles. It lived about 210 million years ago.*

pythons, boas, vipers, rattlesnakes, and their relatives. One member of the boa group called *Madstoia* even reached a length of more than thirty feet.

All snakes are all carnivores and skilled predators. Some kill their prey through constriction and suffocation, whereas others utilize poisonous venom produced by modified saliva glands. In many snakes, the prey is swallowed whole, a procedure that is facilitated by the fact that the lower jaws are very flexibly attached to the skull and to each other making it easy to enlarge the opening of the mouth.

From here, the evolutionary path leads into a group of reptiles called archosaurs, which means "ruling reptiles." Included among the archosaurs are crocodiles, pterosaurs, and dinosaurs, including birds. These animals inherited an opening on the skull in front of the eye socket called the antorbital fenestra. This opening is part of a complex system of air sacks found in the skulls of all archosaurs; the function of these sacks, however, is not clearly understood. Additional evolutionary innovations typical of archosaurs are teeth that fit into sockets in the jaw and an extensively modified jaw joint. These latter features are related to catching and feeding on large prey.

A common theme within archosaur evolution is the development of new types of locomotion. More primitive reptiles possessed a sprawling posture in which the front and hind limbs stuck out from the side of the body before extending down to the ground. However, even the most primitive archosaurs had limbs that were oriented more vertically. This orientation of the limbs may have provided archosaurs with more speed or endurance than earlier sprawling amniotes. In addition, the structure of the ankle was modified. Eventually evolution produced a wide variety of locomotory styles among archosaurs, including the four-footed walking of huge sauropod dinosaurs, the stealthy swimming movements of crocodiles, and even the airborne antics of pterosaurs and birds.

At this point in the hall, crocodiles and their extinct relatives, such as the crocodilelike phytosaurs, branch off the main trunk of the reptilian evolutionary tree. One early relative of living crocodiles and alligators was *Prestosuchus,* an intimidating predator that lived about 200 million years ago in what is now Argentina. The mount portrays the animal in the midst of a charging attack. The enormous skull, with jaws that sported deadly piercing teeth, betray its predatory habits. Nonetheless, this animal is not a dinosaur but rather a distantly related contemporary of the earliest-known dinosaurs.

Prestosuchus is more closely related to living crocodiles and alligators. Although living crocodiles are restricted to aquatic habitats, earlier lineages within the group exploited terrestrial environments. In fact, their remains have been collected on every continent. In living members of the group, diet seems to be correlated with the width of the end of the snout. In broad-muzzled forms, such as crocodiles and alligators, the diet is varied, and prey including fish, turtles, and even terrestrial vertebrates are eaten. In the thin-muzzled forms, such as gavials, the diet is more restricted, and hunting is limited to fish.

Living crocodiles and their close relatives live within a narrow range of climatic conditions. They inhabit temperate and equatorial regions where air temperatures never drop below freezing. Consequently, the presence of crocodilians in ancient faunas has often been used as a clue for interpreting what the temperature was like in past ages. For example, fossils of crocodiles have been found in ancient rocks in Wyoming and even near the present-day Arctic Circle, suggesting that at the end of the Age of Dinosaurs and the beginning of the Age of Mammals climates were much warmer and less seasonal than they are today.

Within the Hall of Vertebrate Origins, the last branch on the evolutionary tree leads to the alcove that contains fossils of the very first flying vertebrates, the pterosaurs. They lived throughout the Mesozoic Era, and their remains, first discovered in 1784, have been found on all continents except Antarctica. Although they were originally interpreted to be related to bats—a group of mammalian flyers—research in the last two centuries has clearly established their reptilian and archosaurian ancestry. Within the context of this exhibition, they are the closest evolutionary relatives of dinosaurs, but they are not dinosaurs themselves. The basis for this interpretation is that pterosaurs and dinosaurs both inherited a unique ankle structure from their common ancestor. It functions like a hinge to consolidate the movements between the bones in the ankle and lower leg, thereby restricting the motions of the foot to a fore-aft plane. This feature may have allowed for increased running speed, although it is difficult to be certain about this. In any event, pterosaurs do not have the hole in the hip socket that was present in the first dinosaur.

In contrast to earlier interpretations in which pterosaurs were thought to be capable of only gliding, they are now thought to have been capable of active, powered flight. Although they do not have a keeled breastbone, as birds do, the wing bones of pterosaurs do exhibit large areas for the attachment of strong flight muscles. In fact, the wings of pterosaurs are constructed quite differently from those of bats and birds. Most of the pterosaur wing is supported only by a bony strut along the front of the wing formed by the elongated bones of the "ring" finger. In contrast, a bird's wing is supported by bones of the entire forearm, and a bat's wing is supported by the bones of all the fingers on the hand. A furlike covering preserved on the wings of some pterosaur specimens suggests that like mammals, the body was thermally insulated, but whether or not pterosaurs were warm-blooded remains a matter of some debate.

Over their long history, pterosaurs evolved into a dizzying array of body forms and sizes. The earliest-known representatives of the group tended to be rather small, such as *Rhamphorhynchus*. The skull supported large eyes, but there was no crest at the back. The optic lobes of the brain were also enlarged, implying enhanced visual acuity, and the areas of the brain that coordinated balance and body movements were also well developed. The elongated jaws were adorned with large

Rhamphorhynchus

sharp teeth that pointed toward the front of the mouth, a feature long-correlated with predators who catch fish. Indeed some *Rhamphorhynchus* fossils have been found with fish bones preserved inside the ribcage. The wing span of this primitive pterosaur was only three feet, and the long tail ended in an oval-shaped, fleshy rudder that presumably helped steer during flight.

In slightly more advanced pterosaurs, such as the diminutive *Pterodactylus,* the tail and rudder were lost. This animal had a wing span of less than a foot; however, its skeletal structure foreshadowed that of the gigantic pterosaurs that would evolve at the end of the Cretaceous. One such form was *Pteranodon,* which sported an enlarged skull with an enormous crest at the back. The skull was constructed of very thin sheets of bone, presumably to help lighten it. The jaws, which formed a long bony beak, were toothless, and fossilized remains of fish and crustaceans have been preserved inside the ribcage of some specimens, providing clues about their diet. The wing span reached at least

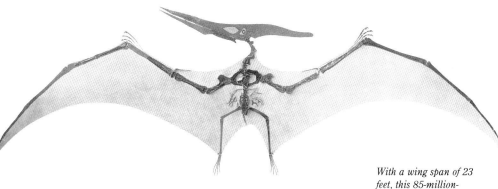

With a wing span of 23 feet, this 85-million-year-old Pteranodon *appears to have been a capable, long distance flyer.*

twenty-three feet in adults, and the wing bones were hollow to help lighten the skeleton, which may have weighed as little as forty pounds. Fossils of these animals have been found in sediments more than one hundred miles from the nearest shoreline of the ancient seaway that cut North America in half at the end of the Cretaceous. So, *Pteranodon* appears to have been a capable, long-distance flyer.

As if involved in some kind of evolutionary arms race, the extreme of pterosaur enormity was not achieved until the end of the Age of Dinosaurs, with the appearance of *Quetzalcoatlus.* To the best of our paleontological knowledge, this was the largest animal ever to take to the skies. Its wing span extended to almost forty feet. Like *Pteranodon,* it had no teeth in its jaws, but unlike *Pteranodon,* it had no crest and does not appear to have inhabited marine environments. Instead, the fossils of *Quetzalcoatlus* are found in flood plain sediments of what is now southern Texas. The diet of this airborne giant remains a mystery.

Our evolutionary journey through this hall has introduced us to the basic building blocks that evolution utilized to construct and reproduce the foundation of the vertebrate body: backbones, jaws, limbs, and the watertight egg. Moving on, we are ready to explore the limbs and branches on the evolutionary tree for the stars of the show, the dinosaurs.

4 ARE ALL DINOSAURS REALLY EXTINCT?

THE HALL OF SAURISCHIAN DINOSAURS

DINOSAURS: THE MAJOR GROUPS AND THEIR EVOLUTIONARY RELATIONSHIPS

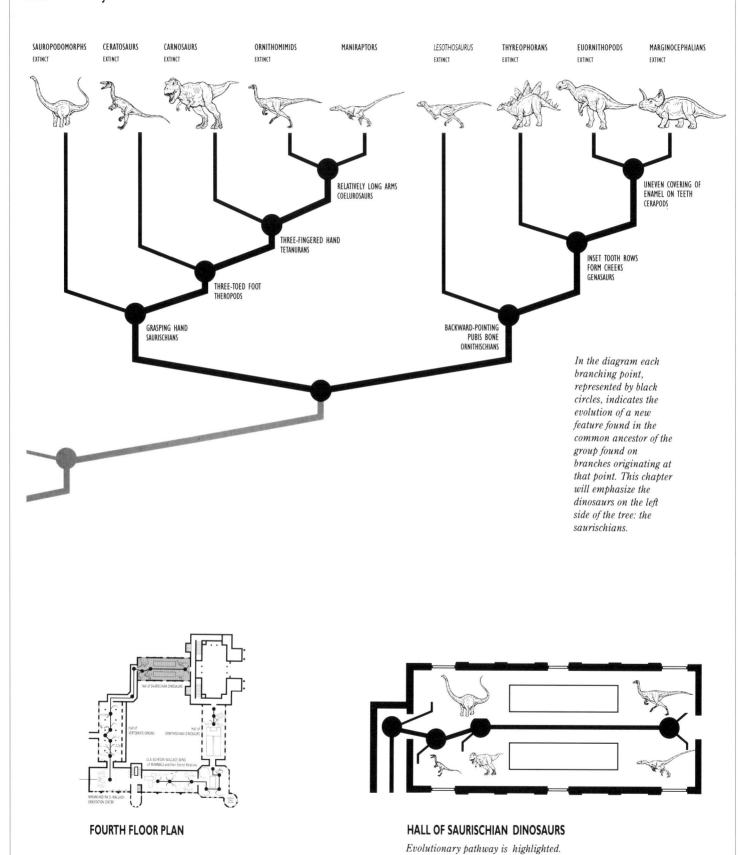

SAUROPODOMORPHS
EXTINCT

CERATOSAURS
EXTINCT

CARNOSAURS
EXTINCT

ORNITHOMIMIDS
EXTINCT

MANIRAPTORS

LESOTHOSAURUS
EXTINCT

THYREOPHORANS
EXTINCT

EUORNITHOPODS
EXTINCT

MARGINOCEPHALIANS
EXTINCT

RELATIVELY LONG ARMS
COELUROSAURS

UNEVEN COVERING OF
ENAMEL ON TEETH
CERAPODS

THREE-FINGERED HAND
TETANURANS

INSET TOOTH ROWS
FORM CHEEKS
GENASAURS

THREE-TOED FOOT
THEROPODS

GRASPING HAND
SAURISCHIANS

BACKWARD-POINTING
PUBIS BONE
ORNITHISCHIANS

*In the diagram each
branching point,
represented by black
circles, indicates the
evolution of a new
feature found in the
common ancestor of the
group found on
branches originating at
that point. This chapter
will emphasize the
dinosaurs on the left
side of the tree: the
saurischians.*

FOURTH FLOOR PLAN

HALL OF SAURISCHIAN DINOSAURS
Evolutionary pathway is highlighted.

I n the bridge that links the end of the Hall of Vertebrate
Origins to the Hall of Saurischian Dinosaurs, visitors
are introduced to the most popular group of vertebrates, the dinosaurs. Dinosaurs have been around for
at least 228 million years, and over that period, they have
evolved into a dazzling array of diverse body forms. An elegant family tree adorned with striking bas-relief sculptures
of representatives from all the major groups makes this
abundantly clear. Some of these models were sculpted
when the dinosaur halls were renovated in the 1950s, but
many new ones have been added as part of this renovation.
Gazing upon the diversity of body forms found in dinosaurs,
one is moved to wonder what formed the basis for this remarkable chapter in evolutionary history.

The story of what makes a dinosaur a dinosaur basically
revolves around locomotion. The common ancestor of dinosaurs possessed a radically different hip structure than
its other reptilian relatives. The hip socket had a hole in the
middle of it, and a strongly developed rim of bone formed
the upper margin of the socket. The result was that dinosaurs inherited a vastly different posture from their common ancestor, as can be seen in a simple comparison.

When lizards stand, their rear limbs extend horizontally
out from the hips before the lower hind limb bones reach
vertically down to the ground. The limbs support the rest of
the body in a sprawling posture, and when the animal
moves, its body basically makes an S-shaped motion. The
hip socket in lizards is solid; in other words, there is no hole
in the middle of it, and if you consider why for a moment, it
seems to make some structural sense. Where the lizard's
upper leg bone meets the hip, a lot of force is generated by
the muscles that pull the bone horizontally into the hip
socket. The hip socket is solid to help resist those horizontally directed forces. No extra bone is needed along the
upper margin to help provide support.

In contrast, dinosaurs have rear limbs that extend vertically straight down to the ground, resulting in a more upright or erect posture in comparison to the sprawling
posture of lizards and other reptiles. Clear evidence of this
posture is found in fossil trackways, which show, for example, that the left and right footprints of the large carnivorous
dinosaur *Allosaurus* form a nearly straight line with one another as the animal walked. With this arrangement of the
rear limbs, the upper limb bone exerted force in a much different direction when it fit into the hip socket. The force
generated by supporting the dinosaur's body was directed
not toward the center of the hip socket but toward the upper margin. In fact, most of the weight of the tail and back
half of the ribcage was hung off the strong bony ridge that
formed the upper rim of the socket. Because little force was
directed toward the center of the hip socket, no bone was
needed to provide support. Hence, a hole is found there.

There is also some evidence to suggest that there may
have been an evolutionary advantage in having the limbs
oriented more vertically. At first glance, one might be
tempted to think that with their more upright posture, dinosaurs could run with longer strides, resulting in greater
speed. Although not all scientists agree, some experiments
measuring the relative speeds of living animals with sprawling and upright postures point out that, over short

This sculptural tree illustrates the relationships of the major groups of dinosaurs.

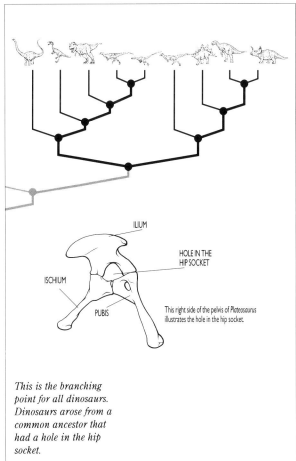

ILIUM

HOLE IN THE
HIP SOCKET

ISCHIUM

PUBIS

This right side of the pelvis of *Plateosaurus*
illustrates the hole in the hip socket.

This is the branching point for all dinosaurs. Dinosaurs arose from a common ancestor that had a hole in the hip socket.

Facing page:
The trackway of an Allosaurus-like dinosaur (far left) shows that the footprints were oriented in a straight line, with one foot falling almost directly in front of the other.

The hind limbs of Apatosaurus (right), like those of other saurischian dinosaurs, extend straight down from its hips.

distances, many sprawlers can actually run as fast as their upright competitors. However, when a sprawler runs, its ribcage is stretched on one side while being constricted on the other, making it impossible to breathe while running. So, whereas sprawlers can run at fast speeds over short distances while holding their breath, their lungs quickly run out of oxygen, and their endurance is not very good.

On the other hand, with their legs swinging in a vertical, fore-aft plane underneath the body, animals with upright posture can run without constricting and stretching the ribcage. This allows them to breathe while they run so that they can run at fast speeds over much greater distances. And therein may lie an important factor in making the 228-million-year lineage of the dinosaur possible. If you picture yourself as potential prey, you may have been faced with a daunting prospect: even if the dinosaur was not faster than you, it could eventually run you down after a long chase.

It is interesting to note that mammals, including you, also possess an erect posture in which our legs extend straight down from the hips. Our hips are built somewhat differently, however. Instead of having three separate bones in the hip, as do dinosaurs, humans have but one, large, fused bone. We also have a solid hip socket. Based on this and a host of other anatomical differences, it appears that our form of upright posture evolved independently from that of dinosaurs.

In terms of specimens, the Hall of Saurischian Dinosaurs contains many of the crown jewels of vertebrate paleontology because saurischians include both the giant sauropods and all the meat-eating theropods.

This hall, located in the thirteenth building to be erected in the museum complex, was designed by the architectural firm of Trowbridge and Livingston and was completed in 1932. The first exhibitions filled what was entitled the Jurassic Dinosaur Hall. Dinosaur collector Barnum Brown served as the curator for the hall, which opened to the public on 18 April 1939. Many popular specimens comprised the roster, including *"Brontosaurus," Allosaurus, Stegosaurus,* and *Plateosaurus.* In addition, representatives from several nondinosaurian groups were displayed in the hallway between the two dinosaur halls, including skeletons of plesiosaurs, mosasaurs, and ichthyosaurs.

The next major renovation took place under the direction of curator Edwin H. Colbert in the early 1950s. Many of the large skeletons were removed, cases redone, and new lighting installed. Colbert supervised major new additions, including a number of chalk drawings around the perimeter walls, specimens of the primitive carnivorous dinosaur, *Coelophysis,* and the sauropod trackway behind the *"Brontosaurus"* mount. A newly built curved base integrated the fossil trackway with the mount. In addition, new nondinosaurian skeletons were added, such as fossil "amphibians," primitive reptiles, and early relatives of mammals (then termed "mammal-like reptiles"). The gallery was called the Jurassic or Brontosaur Hall, although one often hears it referred to as the Hall of Early Dinosaurs. It reopened on 22 May 1953. The Fossil Fish Alcove at the west end of the Early Dinosaur Hall opened on 7 April 1954 to tell the story of "Fishes Through Time."

This same hall now hosts specimens from one of the

The Fossil Fish Alcove (as it was in 1954), which described the evolutionary story of fishes through time, has been expanded into a major part of the Hall of Vertebrate Origins.

Theropod dinosaurs include all saurischians except sauropods and their early relatives The advanced feature of theropods is the

3-TOED hind FOOT

The central 3 toes are large,

while the first and fifth toes are small or absent.

This foot was probably an adaptation prey. The 3-toed foot of me survived as the 3-toed foot of

Having three toes on the hind foot (seen in the display, far right) is an advanced feature of theropod dinosaurs, the group that includes both Tyrannosaurus *and living birds.*

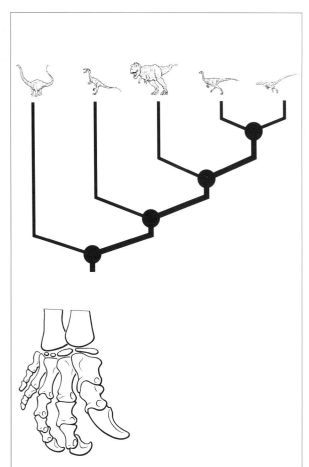

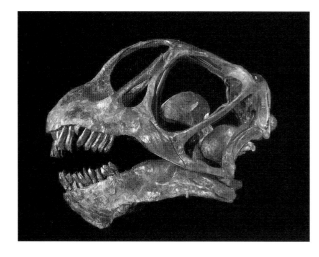

two main branches on the dinosaur family tree, the saurischians. One secret to their evolutionary success is found in the structure of their hand. The fingers are of different lengths, and the thumb is somewhat offset from the other fingers. This results in an arrangement that appears to have allowed most saurischians to have at least a limited capability for grasping. In the main groups of carnivorous dinosaurs, the theropods, this capability was most probably used in conjunction with their previously mentioned endurance for catching prey. But the grasping hand that evolved in the common ancestor of saurischians was eventually adapted to serve some other remarkable functions as well. In the long-necked sauropods, evolution molded a sturdy structure capable of supporting the immense mass of the largest animals ever known to have walked the earth. Within another saurischian lineage leading to living birds, the grasping hand evolved into a wing, capable of freeing some dinosaurs from a completely terrestrial existence. These improbable evolutionary journeys form the focus of this first dinosaur hall.

Greeting visitors as they enter is the reconfigured mount of *Apatosaurus* (once called *Brontosaurus*), the heaviest fossil skeleton in the museum's collection. It represents an important historical milestone in more than simply an evolutionary sense because it was the first complete, large dinosaur mount ever constructed. Since making its public debut back in 1905, this beast has inhabited three halls on the fourth floor. The earliest images of it can be used to document that its original home was in the present Hall of Primitive Mammals. It is hard to imagine being able to squeeze that enormous sixty-six-foot-long body in between the columns of this relatively small hall, but archival photos clearly establish that it was possible. The skeleton was moved into the building it now occupies when the newly built Hall of Early Dinosaurs opened in 1953.

Although Henry Fairfield Osborn and his colleagues used the best information available when the mount was originally constructed, research during subsequent decades has pointed up some things that needed to be changed. Before this renovation project, most ten-year-olds knew that we had the wrong head on the animal. At the time the original mount was built, no one knew what the skull or tail of *Apatosaurus* really looked like because no fossils of these elements had ever been found. As a guess, Osborn and his colleagues furnished the mount with a tall vaulted skull and a relatively short tail, because Osborn believed that *Apatosaurus* was closely related to the small, stout sauropod named *Camarasaurus*.

In the 1970s, however, it became clear from further collecting and research that *Apatosaurus* was more closely related to the long, lithe sauropod called *Diplodocus* and that it had a long low skull and whiplike tail more like that of *Diplodocus* than *Camarasaurus*. The primary consultant on our remounting project, Jack McIntosh, played a leading role in correcting the earlier misconceptions. In truth, we have still not found an apatosaur skeleton with the skull directly attached to the neck. However, one long tapering sauropod skull, resembling that of *Diplodocus,* was found just a few feet from the end of an apatosaur neck, and that skull fits snugly on the last neck vertebra. At this point, that

The Apatosaurus *in its original installation in 1921, in what is now the Lila Acheson Wallace Wing of Mammals and their Extinct Relatives.*

*Looking down the
evolutionary pathway in
the Hall of Saurischian
Dinosaurs,* Tyrannosaurus
is on the left and

skull represents our best guess about how the skull of Apatosaurus really looked. Many museums have now removed the old skull on their apatosaur mounts and substituted a cast of that new skull.

In the 1970s, the curator then in charge of the American Museum of Natural History's dinosaur collection, Eugene Gaffney, tried to bring our mount up to current paleontological code, but in the process of trying to remove the skull, vibrations transmitted down along the supporting metal framework, or armature, damaged some of the ribs. Consequently, he quite rightly decided to wait until a more thorough job of reconstruction could be done.

In reality, that job required more than just changing the skull. If the new skull were to be stuck directly on the end of the old neck, the apatosaur would have looked quite silly—kind of pin-headed. Consequently, four vertebrae had to be added to the neck in order to provide the correct number, and the length of the tail had to be increased substantially. As a result of these changes, the mount is now about eighty-six feet long rather than the original length of about sixty-six feet.

Remounting the Apatosaurus involved the efforts of all three crews in the renovation group. Under the direction of Steven Warsavage, the installation crew built an intricate, two-story-tall, wooden structure completely around the old mount to stabilize it and to create platforms from which to work. The preparation crew, under the direction of Jeanne Kelly, conducted a detailed inspection of the fossil bones, identifying where cracks had developed over the decades and injecting epoxy into the weak spots. At that point, the mount was ready for partial disassembly, an operation handled by the mount-making crew under the direction of Phil Fraley. Bone by bone, the skull and neck vertebrae were taken off the supporting metal armature, and the tail was similarly disassembled. As a result, only the torso remained on a large wooden base supported by the original castors. Although the seventeen-ton skeleton was ready to move, that was only half the problem. In addition to the fossil bones, the apatosaur exhibit also incorporates a real fossil trackway that includes sauropod footprints mixed in with those of a large carnivorous dinosaur. The responsibility for moving these fragile, yet weighty, fossils fell to the installation crew. Buttressed by the supporting scaffolding and cables, the ninety-year-old base was rolled around into its new position with little difficulty.

But the trackway proved to be more of a challenge. In total, the trackway weighs twenty-two tons and is composed of several separate blocks of rock that contain the individual footprints. When the Hall of Early Dinosaurs was originally put together, Colbert had called its collector, Roland T. Bird, out of retirement to oversee the reassembly of the individual blocks into a reconstructed trackway. All the individual blocks were plastered together. The trackway, which was discovered in the bed of the Paluxy River in Texas, was never intended to be transported anywhere. Instead of completely disassembling it before moving it to its new location, Steve Warsavage and his crew knew it would be easier if they could figure out a way to move it as one piece. Their ingenious plan called for reversing an old magic trick. As Steve described it:

Preparators reassemble the trackway of a sauropod dinosaur in 1952, which was discovered in the bed of the Paluxy River in Texas.

The graceful
Apatosaurus *with its*
sinuous, whiplike tail
waving in its wake.

The three-toed hind foot is an advanced feature of theropod dinosaurs, the group that includes Tyrannosaurus *and* Allosaurus. *The central toe is large, while the outside toes are reduced or lost. This arrangement is the same as that found in birds.*

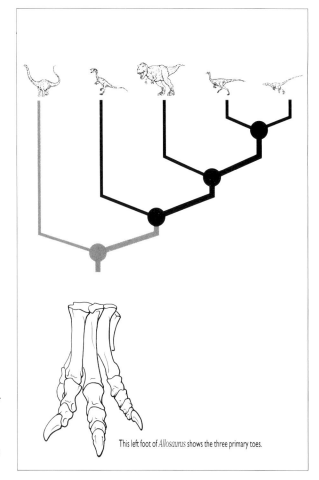

This left foot of *Allosaurus* shows the three primary toes.

Below: Coelophysis *is one of the earliest known theropod dinosaurs.*

Bottom: *Inside the stomach cavity of this* Coelophysis *are bones of a juvenile* Coelophysis. *These specimens suggest that* Coelophysis *occasionally cannibalized its young.*

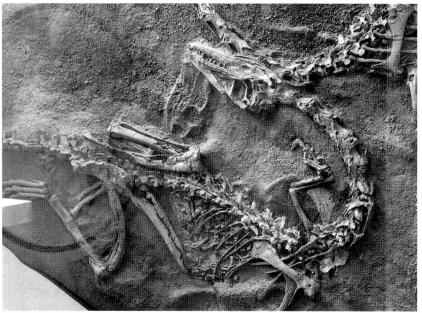

First, we got thick steel plates, beveled the front of them, coated their bottoms with molybdenum grease, and drove them underneath the trackway blocks. You've seen how magicians pull a tablecloth out from underneath the silverware and plates? Well, this was like putting the tablecloth back underneath without disturbing the plates and silverware.

Then, with long steel cables secured to the entrances at the opposite ends of the halls, the whole block was winched around and moved into its new position.

With the skeleton and the trackway safely in place, the mount-makers once again took over. This crew contained a group of master artisans and technicians. In hiring members for this group, Phil Fraley drew heavily from New York's art community. Mount-makers must be especially adept in working with metals, a critical skill for bending and welding the framework that supports the fossil bones. Working with the paleontologists, mount-makers develop sketches or scale models of the proposed mount to help define the form and posture. Once a consensus is reached, months of work are required to bend and construct the metal armature before attaching the fragile skeleton. Although many inferences and assumptions must be made about how the animal moved when it was alive, what emerges is a stunningly dynamic image of a long-vanished organism.

Fraley and his colleagues took about six months to rebuild the apatosaur's neck and tail. Although many would disagree, this is my favorite mount in the halls. The level of dynamic animation they achieved is truly incredible. Although the apatosaur probably weighed between twenty and thirty tons when it was alive, the mount depicts an amazingly graceful and gracile animal. It appears to be ambling effortlessly through the hall, just as it probably walked across the 140-million-year-old flood plains of the Jurassic, with its sinuous, whiplike tail waving in its wake.

Across the hall from the apatosaur, visitors can follow the branches of the evolutionary tree that lead to the alcoves containing the different groups of carnivorous dinosaurs, called theropods. These animals, which include the largest predators ever to have walked the land, evolved from a common ancestor that had a foot composed of three well-developed toes that point toward the front of the animal and one small toe that occupies the same position as our big toe.

The earliest-known representative of theropods in the hall is the 220-million-year-old ceratosaur called *Coelophysis*. The first fossils of this animal were discovered by Edwin H. Colbert, the curator of the dinosaur collections at the museum when the Halls of Early and Late Dinosaurs were being developed in the 1950s. Colbert and his colleague, George Whitaker, discovered a rich bone bed of *Coelophysis* remains at a locality in New Mexico named Ghost Ranch. The locality has yielded the remains of hundreds of individuals, including adults and juveniles, suggesting that the animals may have died as the result of a catastrophe such as a flash flood or a drought.

The two skeletons on exhibit are displayed as they were found, with the neck and head arched back over the body.

A case in front of Apatosaurus highlights the comparison between its former skull, which resembles that of Camarasaurus, *and the new skull, similar to that of its close relative* Diplodocus.

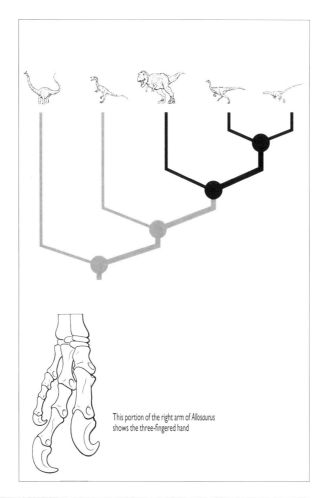

This portion of the right arm of *Allosaurus* shows the three-fingered hand

The Allosaurus, *mounted in 1908, is shown as if feeding on the backbone of an* Apatosaurus.

This is a common mode of preservation for fossil skeletons. It probably represents a death pose which resulted from the ligaments in the neck shrinking as the carcass of the dead animal dried out. What is uncommon about these skeletons is what was discovered inside the rib cages of the two adults, the tiny bones of juvenile *Coelophysis.* These were originally interpreted to be the bones of unborn young; further research, however, has made it clear that a more grizzly explanation is more likely: *Coelophysis* was, at least to some degree, cannibalistic, sometimes feeding on the young of its own species.

A bit farther down the main path, visitors encounter the branching point at which carnivorous dinosaurs evolved a hand with three or fewer fingers. These dinosaurs belong to a group called tetanurans, and the first branch to diverge from this branching point leads to the largest terrestrial carnivores of all time, the carnosaurs.

An island along the south side of the hall constitutes the new home for the world's two most famous carnosaurs, *Allosaurus* and *Tyrannosaurus.* Interestingly, both mounts depict these huge animals in very dynamic postures, as is common in contemporary exhibitions; however, the allosaur mount was completed in 1908. The specimen was discovered in 1879 by a collector working for dinosaur paleontologist Edward Drinker Cope. The museum purchased the Cope collection after the scientist's death in 1899, and work soon began on the preparation and mounting of the skeleton. The mount shows *Allosaurus* feeding on the carcass of *Apatosaurus,* its 140-million-year-old contemporary. The scene was inspired by the fact that some of the vertebrae in the apatosaur skeleton had deep linear gouges inscribed into them, and broken teeth of an allosaur were preserved adjacent to the apatosaur backbone. Consequently, Osborn and his colleagues reasoned that the scratch marks were probably made by either the teeth or the claws of a large carnosaur.

Comparing the skeletons of *Allosaurus* and its younger cousin *Tyrannosaurus* makes clear some trends within carnosaur evolution. Between 140 million and 65 million years ago, the carnosaur skull, already disproportionately large in *Allosaurus,* evolved into an enormous structure with jaws built like meat cleavers. In contrast, the arms decreased in size. In fact, the easiest way to tell an allosaur from a tyrannosaur is to look at the number of fingers. *Allosaurus* has three, whereas *Tyrannosaurus* has only two.

In addition to the partial renovation of the *Apatosaurus,* the other major project handled by the renovation crews involved the disassembly and remounting of our skeleton of *Tyrannosaurus rex.* This specimen is, without question, the most famous dinosaur fossil in the world. Collected around 1908 in Montana by the museum's Barnum Brown, the specimen included the first skull of *Tyrannosaurus* ever found.

On one of the tours leading up to the opening of the dinosaur halls, someone asked me if I had a pet name for the tyrannosaur. At first, the question struck me as being rather silly. To me, neither Mable nor even Rex sounds very appropriate. But despite my continued reference to it by its generic name, I have developed a certain emotional tie to this animal because the fossil skeleton provides several windows into this individual's life.

FOSSIL FISHES

The Allosaurus *on*
display in 1911.

In the new dinosaur halls the 140-million-year-old Allosaurus *bends over its meal…*

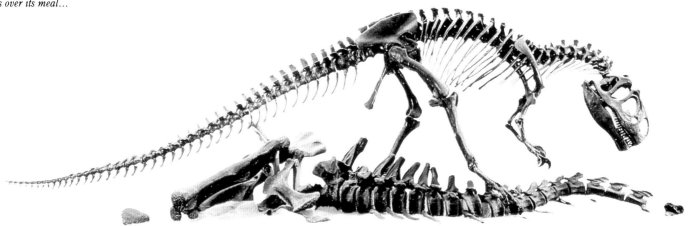

...while the 65-million-year-old Tyrannosaurus *prepares to lunge forward toward its prey.*

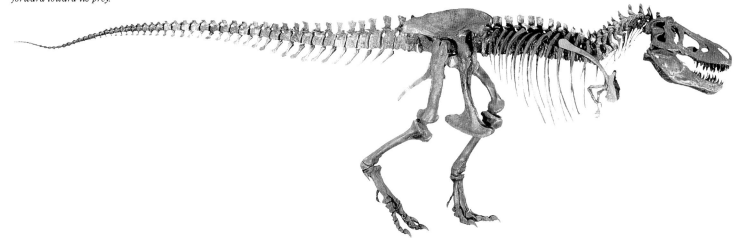

Top: *For the new mount of* Tyrannosaurus, *skilled metalworkers sculpted individual cradles for each vertebra in the backbone.*

Bottom: *The construction of the new mount involved the careful positioning of each large and extremely fragile bone to achieve the riveting new pose.*

Our tyrannosaur was probably a nasty old codger. As part of this renovation, Jeanne Kelly's preparation crew did an exquisite job of preparing each individual neck bone out of the rocky matrix in which the skeleton had been entombed—a job that had not been completed when the skeleton was originally assembled. Close examination revealed a fusion between the two neck vertebrae that form the bottom of the curve where the neck is joined to the rib cage. In addition, two more rib-bearing vertebrae are fused together farther back along the spine. At this point, it is not entirely clear what caused these fusions. Perhaps they represent the result of an injury, an arthritic condition, or even a form of bone cancer. But whatever the cause, the result must have been both painful and, at least to some degree, debilitating. What is more, the animal clearly suffered a couple of broken ribs at some point in its life, judging by the lumps of bone that were deposited where the ribs healed. Although popular wisdom suggests that tyrannosaurs could do whatever they pleased, life was clearly not always a bed of roses for this tyrant king of the Cretaceous.

Because of the bones' fragility, it required an average of four people working for a year and a half to complete the remounting of the tyrannosaur skeleton. Most of the bones in the vertebral column, hips, and ribs are real fossils. First, as with the apatosaur, the skeleton had to be inspected, the fossils reprepared and stabilized, and the mount disarticulated. As Kelly and her crew proceeded with this work, Phil Fraley's mounting crew, working closely with Gene Gaffney and the primary curator for this hall, Mark Norell, began to develop a design for the new pose. A scale model was built using small cast bones from the carved wooden model that Henry Fairfield Osborn and Barnum Brown had used to develop the original pose. That mount had the animal standing erect, with its head nearly twenty feet in the air and the tail dragging along the ground behind it.

The new mount features a more horizontal pose, with the skull down and the tail up off the ground to counterbalance the weight of the head and torso. This posture is similar to that of cursorial birds, such as the roadrunner, in which the head is held low when the animal sprints after prey, and the tail feathers act as a stiff rudder that sticks straight out behind the body. The effect of the new pose is designed to give visitors a rather riveting, face-to-face sense of what it might have been like to be stalked by this magnificent predator.

Across the main path from the tyrannosaur, a short time-lapse video documents the stages in the construction of the new mount. Phil Fraley and his crew first fabricated the major elements of the armature for the hips and hind legs, and sculpted the individual cradles that held each vertebra in the backbone. Then, they finished the construction of the rib cage and mounted all the elements on the armature. Finally, the preparators painstakingly painted the cast bones to bring out the real color of the fossils.

At the last branching point in this hall, one group of theropods, called coelurosaurs, evolved elongated arms. In most of these animals, these long arms, coupled with the grasping hands inherited from the common ancestor of all saurischians, were probably used to great advantage in catching prey.

The Tyrannosaurus as displayed in its former, more erect, pose, in 1927.

Near the entrance to the Hall of Saurischian Dinosaurs the new head of Apatosaurus (*with its corrected skull*) *looms over the skeleton of* Allosaurus.

allosaurs and tyrannosaurs

CARNOSAURS

The largest carnivorous animals ever to walk on land were the carnosaurs. They had huge claws and they walked on their rear legs. Carnosaur skeletons have been collected on every continent.

an enlarged opening on the side of the lacrimal

The largest carnivorous animals ever to walk on land were the carnosaurs. They had huge claws and they walked on their rear legs. Carnosaur skeletons have been collected on every continent. All carnosaurs have

an enlarged opening on the side of the lacrimal

the bone of the upper front corner of the eye. Other theropod dinosaurs lack this opening. Much remains to be learned about carnosaurs, and some of our views about their evolutionary relationships with other theropods will probably change.

The 3-fingered hand

the common ancestor of

TETANURANS

Coelurosaurs is a group that includes the "bird-mimic" ornithomimids as well as maniraptors such as Velociraptor *and birds. Ceolurosaurs have relatively long arms, which may have been used to capture prey and have been evolutionarily modified into wings for flight in birds.*

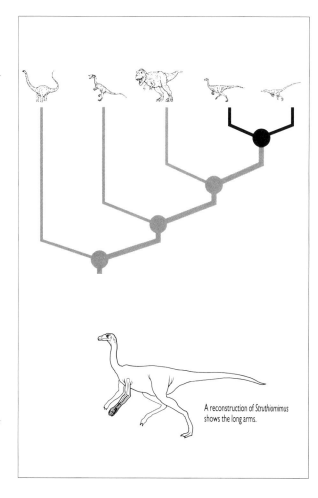

A reconstruction of *Struthiomimus* shows the long arms.

Struthiomimus, *a toothless ornithomimid dinosaur, was nonetheless probably an agile and speedy predator; it lived in North America about 75 million years ago.*

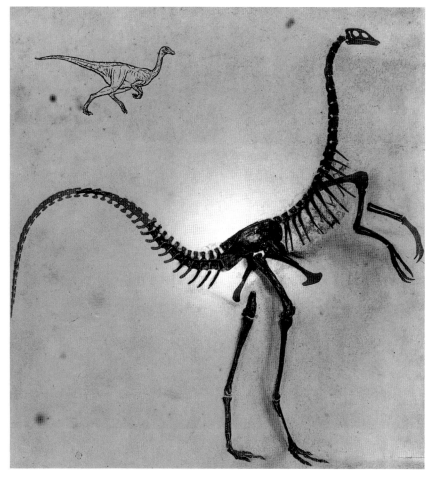

On one limb diverging from this branching point is the alcove for the bird-mimic or ostrich dinosaurs. Although these animals are not really birds, their general body proportions are very reminiscent of birds' proportions. In addition to having long arms, ornithomimids possessed long necks, long legs, large brains, and enormous eyes. All these features seem to point to an agile, swift animal adapted for hunting, except for one curious feature. Only the most primitive ornithomimids had any teeth; the more advanced forms were completely toothless. Instead, their sharp, bird-like beaks were probably covered with a horny sheath. Even without teeth, however, it is likely that ornithomimids were skillful hunters. Can you think of any highly successful modern predators that do not have teeth? If not, you can find some right across the main path in the adjacent alcove.

The last branch of the evolutionary tree in this hall features a recent realization: dinosaurs are not really extinct! We are not talking about alleged denizens of Loch Ness or the jungles of the Congo; we are talking about animals outside your own window. It is true that *Apatosaurus* and *Tyrannosaurus* have been extinct for millions of years, but over the last two decades, evolutionary research has established beyond much doubt that birds evolved from some small carnivorous dinosaur.

The skeletal similarities between the first known bird, *Archaeopteryx,* and other small theropods, such as *Velociraptor,* are overwhelming. This is made clear by examining some of the very unusual specimens exhibited in this alcove. Our mount of *Deinonychus* is the only one in the world that contains any real fossils. This animal is a close North American relative of *Velociraptor,* the small Asian predator made famous through its larger-than-life appearance in the science fiction movie *Jurassic Park.* In addition, the alcove features casts of all the most important specimens of the earliest-known bird, *Archaeopteryx.*

By looking for features shared by *Archaeopteryx* and other dinosaurs, we can trace the sequence of evolution from the origin of birds all the way back to the origin of dinosaurs. For example, *Deinonychus* and *Velociraptor* even had a wishbone, formed by fused collar bones, just as living birds do. They also had a wrist that was built around a bone called the semilunate carpal, which, as the name implies, is shaped like a half moon. Some paleontologists have even gone so far as to argue that because of the similarities in the wrist structure, the grasping motion of dinosaurs like *Velociraptor* and *Deinonychus* was very similar to the flying motion of the wings in early birds like *Archaeopteryx.* Whether or not this is true, it is clear that a wishbone and a half-moon-shaped wrist bone were present in the common ancestor of birds and these little carnivorous dinosaurs.

If we look back a little farther down the evolutionary tree, we can see that birds inherited their hollow bones from their common ancestor with *Allosaurus* and *Tyrannosaurus.* Hollow bones had long been thought to be a unique characteristic of birds related to the evolution of a lighter skeleton for flight, but if one examines the bones of *Tyrannosaurus,* one finds that they, too, are hollow. This feature may once have served to lighten up the skeleton in order to make the more advanced predatory dinosaurs more agile. In addition, the foot of *Tyrannosaurus* is almost a deadringer

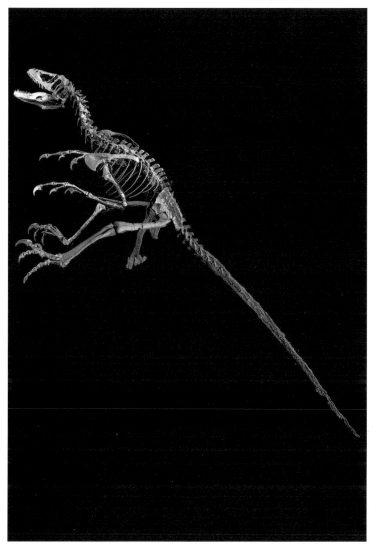

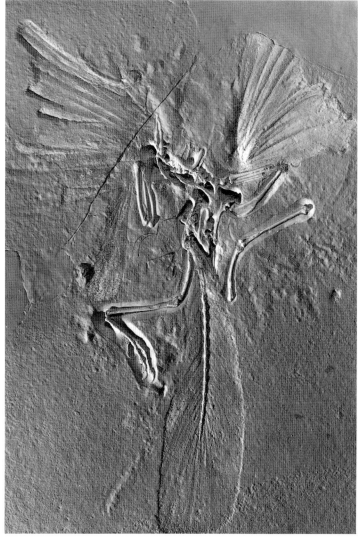

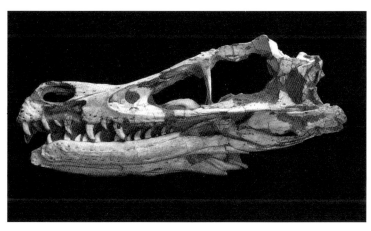

Above left:
Deinonychus, *a 110-million-year-old maniraptor closely related to* Velociraptor *from Asia, was a comparatively intelligent, agile predator.*

Above: Archaeopteryx *is the earliest known bird. Here you can see the impression of its feathers preserved in the limestone matrix that settled on the bottom of a 140-million-year-old sea in Europe.*

Left: Velociraptor *is a Mongolian dinosaur that lived about 72 million years ago; its name means "swift robber."*

These pictures show the largest mounts in their new home, the Hall of Saurischian Dinosaurs, under construction—the newly refurbished Tyrannosaurus *(top left)*, Allosaurus *(bottom left)*, Apatosaurus *(top right)*, and Tyrannosaurus *(bottom right)*, seen over the tail of Apatosaurus.

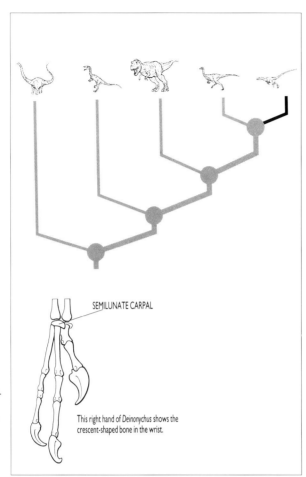

Maniraptors share a crescent-shaped wrist called the semilunate carpal that was inherited from their yet-to-be-discovered common ancestor. This feature is found in its descendants, such as Deinonychus *(below right)*, and birds.

SEMILUNATE CARPAL

This right hand of *Deinonychus* shows the crescent-shaped bone in the wrist.

for that of a bird, with three large toes pointing forward and one small toe on the inner side of the foot pointing backward. Birds also inherited the hole in the hip socket that evolved in the common ancestor of all dinosaurs. As a result, they walk around on hind legs that extend vertically down from the hips, just like all other dinosaurs.

These and a host of other features establish that birds evolved from some dinosaur that probably looked a lot like *Velociraptor* and *Deinonychus* but that lived much earlier. Since the fossil record is incomplete, we have yet to find fossils of this common ancestor. Nonetheless, given all this anatomical evidence, the most reasonable interpretation of the fossil record is that birds are really part of the dinosaur "family" in an evolutionary sense. In other words, birds are not separated from dinosaurs; they are simply dinosaurs that evolved feathers and the ability to fly. This means that you do not have to wait for a real Jurassic Park to be built in order see living dinosaurs; after you visit the exhibits at the museum, you can go out and feed them in Central Park!

This realization that birds are living dinosaurs actually resolves another heated debate about dinosaur physiology: Were they warm-blooded or cold-blooded? Since birds are still alive, we can measure their body temperature and conclude, without any doubt, that some dinosaurs are warm-blooded. Because crocodiles are cold-blooded, it is clear that warm-bloodedness evolved within the dinosaurian lineage sometime between the point that crocodiles branched off on the evolutionary tree for reptiles and the point that birds evolved. We can bracket the origin of warm-bloodedness in this way because crocodiles are the closest living relatives of dinosaurs outside the group itself, and birds belong to the group. We still cannot be sure, however, just when within the dinosaurian lineage that warm-bloodedness evolved. It may well be that on-going studies examining the cellular structure of dinosaur bone eventually resolve this issue. But for now, the question of whether *Tyrannosaurus* and *Apatosaurus* were warm-blooded remains a mystery.

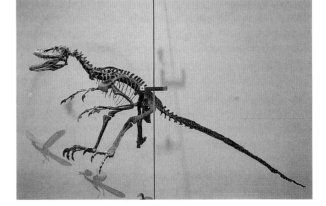

Deinonychus *has a wrist structure very similar to that found in early birds. Some paleontologists believe that the grasping motion of such dinosaurs was similar to the flying motion of early birds.*

Facing page: *Dinosaurs are still alive! Living birds evolved from some dinosaurs whose skeletons probably looked a lot like* Velociraptor *and* Deinonychus.

When Stegosaurus
was first described
by the paleontologist
O. C. Marsh
in the 1890s,
Marsh placed emphasis
on the animal's
small brain cavity
and the expansion
of the spinal cord in the pelvis.
This gave rise
to the completely incorrect idea
that dinosaurs were
so unintelligent
that they needed
a second "brain"
to control the movements
of their hindlimbs,
back, and tail.

Did Stegosaurus Have 2 Brains?

In fact, most vertebrates have an expansion of the spinal cord in the pelvis, at the place where nerves from the back legs and tail come together. Larger animals, such as elephants, have large expansions. Because many dinosaurs were large, the expansion in the spinal cord was also large. But Stegosaurus did not have 2 brains!

THYRE

5 THE EXIT OF LARGE DINOSAURS:

Backward-
pointing
EXTENSION
of
PUBIS BONE

The hip structure of ornithischian dinosaurs
in relation to
that of
saurischians.

Because this arrangement of hip bone
was origin...

CENASAURS

THE HALL OF ORNITHISCHIAN DINOSAURS

DINOSAURS: THE MAJOR GROUPS AND THEIR EVOLUTIONARY RELATIONSHIPS

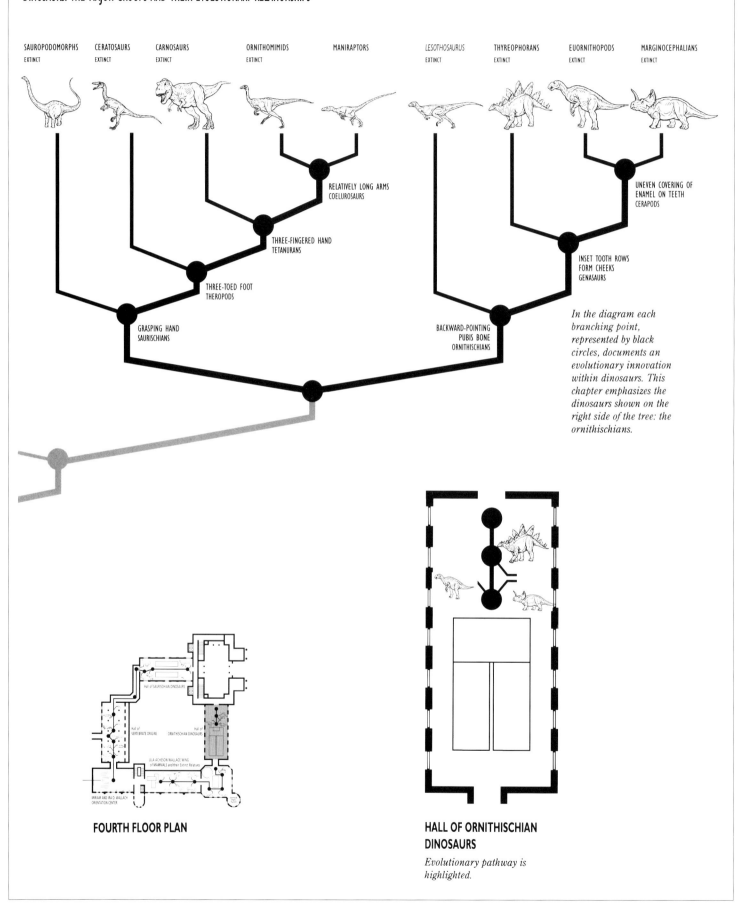

SAUROPODOMORPHS
EXTINCT

CERATOSAURS
EXTINCT

CARNOSAURS
EXTINCT

ORNITHOMIMIDS
EXTINCT

MANIRAPTORS

LESOTHOSAURUS
EXTINCT

THYREOPHORANS
EXTINCT

EUORNITHOPODS
EXTINCT

MARGINOCEPHALIANS
EXTINCT

RELATIVELY LONG ARMS
COELUROSAURS

THREE-FINGERED HAND
TETANURANS

THREE-TOED FOOT
THEROPODS

GRASPING HAND
SAURISCHIANS

UNEVEN COVERING OF
ENAMEL ON TEETH
CERAPODS

INSET TOOTH ROWS
FORM CHEEKS
GENASAURS

BACKWARD-POINTING
PUBIS BONE
ORNITHISCHIANS

*In the diagram each
branching point,
represented by black
circles, documents an
evolutionary innovation
within dinosaurs. This
chapter emphasizes the
dinosaurs shown on the
right side of the tree: the
ornithischians.*

FOURTH FLOOR PLAN

**HALL OF ORNITHISCHIAN
DINOSAURS**

*Evolutionary pathway is
highlighted.*

The second dinosaur hall contains a remarkably diverse group, called ornithischians, that comprise the other main branch on the dinosaurs' family tree. Many of the most popular dinosaurs belong to this group, including stegosaurs, ankylosaurs, hadrosaurs, ceratopsians, and pachycephalosaurs. All these dinosaurs evolved from a common ancestor with an extension on one of its hip bones, the pubis, that points toward the rear of the animal. It is not immediately obvious just what, if any, evolutionary advantage this arrangement conveyed on ornithischians; however, it is a feature generally shared by members of the group.

The different kinds of ornithischians sport a spectacular variety of bony ornamentation, including spikes of armor, elaborate crests, enormous horns, and bony helmets. Our intent is to use these commonly recognized features to discuss the array of speculations about dinosaur behavior as well as the group's evolutionary fate.

The ornithischians now occupy the ninth building constructed in the museum's physical plant. It was completed in 1922. The architectural design was developed by the firm of Trowbridge and Livingston. Coined "The Great Dinosaur Hall," Henry Fairfield Osborn intended it to be the third in a series of six halls portraying life from its origins to the present. I suspect that he was referring to the same six halls that comprise the spatial scope of the present renovation, although now these six halls are limited to telling the story of vertebrate evolution. The line-up included *Tyrannosaurus, "Trachodon"* (now called *Anatotitan*), *"Brontosaurus," Allosaurus,* and *Triceratops,* as well as newcomers such as *Thescelosaurus* and *Leptoceratops.*

The next renovation was not attempted until the mid-1950s, after Colbert and his staff completed the Hall of Early Dinosaurs. Besides the application of a fresh coat of paint and installation of new lighting, a new center island was created to integrate the mounts of the *"Trachodon," Tyrannosaurus,* and *Triceratops.* Newly added were displays of *Protoceratops* fossils and of pterosaurs, the closest relatives of dinosaurs. These new exhibits were opened to the public on 25 July 1956 under the title The Cretaceous or Tyrannosaur Hall, which was also often called the Hall of Late Dinosaurs.

Because we chose to rearrange the halls based on the evolutionary relationships, many of the large specimens had to be carefully moved into the hall with their closest cousins. Such was the case for our skeleton of *Stegosaurus.* In the earlier arrangement of halls, it stood alongside the *Apatosaurus* skeleton in the Hall of Early Dinosaurs. Over the years, many of the original bones had been replaced with cast bones for security purposes. As part of this recent renovation, however, most of the real bones have been put back on the *Stegosaurus* mount, including many real plates along the vertebral column and the spikes near the back of the tail.

Features such as these plates and spikes are eternally intriguing to paleontologists and public alike. What purpose did they serve? Questions like this continually arise within the context of studying extinct animals, especially dinosaurs. When it comes to dinosaur behavior, imaginations tend to run wild. In essence, dinosaurs are at least as

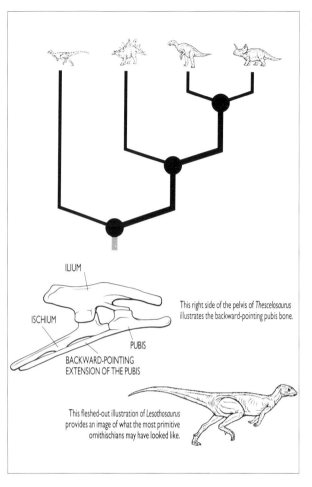

ILIUM

ISCHIUM

PUBIS

BACKWARD-POINTING
EXTENSION OF THE PUBIS

This right side of the pelvis of *Thescelosaurus* illustrates the backward-pointing pubis bone.

This fleshed-out illustration of *Lesothosaurus* provides an image of what the most primitive ornithischians may have looked like.

All ornithischian dinosaurs inherited a backward-pointing extension of the pubis bone from their common ancestor.

The mounted bones of an adult Stegosaurus *loom large over a reconstruction of a juvenile* Stegosaurus *at its side.*

Inset
TOOTH ROWS
form
CHEEKS

pachycephalosaurs
and ceratopsians
MARGINOCEPHALIANS

*Armored ornithischians
are called thyreophorans,
a diverse group that
includes stegosaurs and
ankylosaurs.*

In 1927 the Great Dinosaur Hall was dominated by the skeletons of (from left to right) Allosaurus, Apatosaurus, *and two* Anatotitan. *Today it is called the Hall of Ornithischian Dinosaurs.*

Facing page: *In the 1950s Tyrannosaurus was also displayed in the hall that is now the Hall of Ornithischian Dinosaurs. It stands here next to the skeleton of* Triceratops.

In the new fossil halls visitors can touch real dinosaur bone, such as this plate of *Stegosauru*

Facing page: An Anatotitan, *a duckbill dinosaur that lived in North America about 65 million years ago, grazes peacefully while its fellow keeps watch.*

Touch
the real thing –
a 140-million-
year-old
Stegosaurus
plate!

Stegosaur
plates,
arranged
in a
double row
down
the back,
may have
been used
for defense
or display.

plate
Stegosaurus stenops
(steg·o·so·rus stEn·ops)
"roofed reptile"
Late Jurassic, 140 million years ago
AMNH 5757, collected by M. P. Hubbell, 1880.
Quarry #4, Aurora, Wyoming

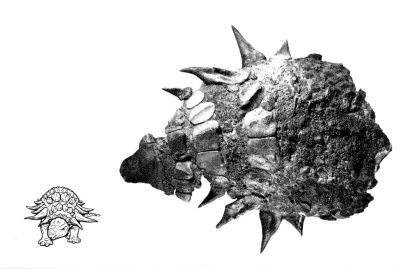

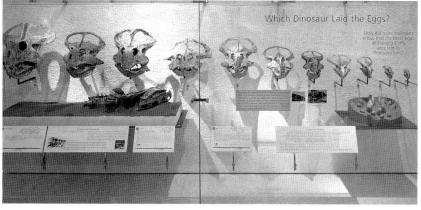

Which Dinosaur Laid the Eggs?

How did paleontologists know that the fossil eggs at Flaming Cliffs were laid by *Protoceratops*?

Top: This top view of the ankylosaur Edmontonia *illustrates the elaborate covering of bony armor found on this 75-million-year-old herbivore.*

Bottom: The Museum's wealth of fossil material made it possible to display a whole series of Protoceratops *skulls, which document the growth of this animal from infancy to adulthood.*

strange as any fiction we can imagine, but they really lived. The fossils prove it. Since dinosaurs are so intriguing, we naturally want to know everything about them. Fossils are good for answering some of our questions, such as how large the animals were and which ones were close evolutionary relatives, but fossils do not provide us with unequivocal answers for all the questions we have. This is a very difficult circumstance for us to accept, whether you are a professional paleontologist or an interested amateur. But if we are going to present things scientifically, we must be honest about the limits of our knowledge. Under the guidance of Mark Norell and the primary curator for this hall, Eugene Gaffney, we have intentionally tried to rein in the speculation a bit by addressing what we do and do not know about stegosaur plates, ankylosaur armor, duckbill crests, ceratopsian horns, and pachycephalosaur skull caps. In each of these instances, the point is to present the speculations that have been proposed, as well as the limitations of the evidence supporting competing points of view. These limitations are often presented on labels designed to look like the Surgeon General's warning labels on cigarette packs. They serve as our warning against blindly accepting over-enthusiastic speculation that is only poorly supported by the fossil evidence.

It is especially difficult to answer questions about how dinosaurs behaved and how some of their more bizarre skeletal structures functioned because all dinosaurs except birds are extinct and we cannot go out and directly observe how they behave. This may seem like a trivial point; however, you would be surprised how many paleontologists, in their eagerness to satisfy their own curiosity as well as that of the public, lose sight of this basic limitation. The resulting speculations about how dinosaurs behaved and functioned cannot be tested scientifically with the available fossil evidence. It may be fun, but it is not really science because scientists limit themselves to asking questions that can be tested with the evidence that they can gather.

In this exhibition, we have tried to introduce some skepticism and to engage the public in an exercise of discovering what we really know about these intriguing relics of evolutionary history. Where speculation abounds, we have laid out the different ideas and discussed why we cannot reach a consensus conclusion. For controversial scientific issues, we have explained the evidence used to support and refute the competing points of view so that visitors can make up their own minds about the questions at hand.

Take the plates and spikes of *Stegosaurus,* for example. These features alone inform us that this animal belongs to a group of ornithischians—the thyreophorans—that inherited an elaborate covering of bony armor from its common ancestor. Other members of this group include the tanklike ankylosaurs and nodosaurs, which are also represented by awe-inspiring specimens in this alcove. By all appearances, the bony armor of thyreophorans primarily served a purpose in defending these animals against the attacks of predators such as *Allosaurus,* in the case of the 140-million-year-old *Stegosaurus,* and *Albertosaurus,* in the case of the 75-million-year-old *Ankylosaurus.* But were *Stegosaurus* plates for defensive purposes?

We know from virtually complete skeletons of

Stegosaurus that the thickened bases of the plates were embedded in the skin, forming a pattern of plates that alternated from one side to the other down the back. Scientists long assumed that the plates did serve a defensive purpose. The surface of the plates, however, are crisscrossed with grooves for blood vessels, indicating that they were covered with skin when the animal was alive. This led some paleontologists to speculate that the plates may have been used as temperature control devices, cooling the blood when the animal was in the shade and warming it when the animal was in the sunlight. Unfortunately, the fossils do not provide us with enough evidence to solve this mystery. Because stegosaurs are extinct, we cannot go out and observe how they used their plates or measure their body temperature.

Although there are limits to our knowledge, we have not stopped learning about dinosaurs. In fact, new fossil skeletons, and even new kinds of dinosaurs, are discovered every year. Several of the most important recent discoveries were made within the group of dinosaurs called cerapods. This group includes the horned dinosaurs or ceratopsians, the bone-headed dinosaurs or pachycephalosaurs, and the duckbills along with their early relatives, the euornithopods. These groups arose from a common ancestor with an unequal covering of enamel on the inside and outside surfaces of its teeth. Like other reptiles, dinosaurs replaced their teeth continually throughout their life, and in many cerapods, a complex mosaic of teeth grew in, one on top of the other, to form an elaborate, rasplike surface for slicing or shredding vegetation. These tooth mosaics are referred to as dental batteries.

One discovery made by paleontologists from this museum documented how dinosaurs entered the world. In the 1920s, explorer and naturalist Roy Chapman Andrews led several AMNH expeditions to Central Asia to collect both living and fossil animals. The crew's most famous discovery was made at the Flaming Cliffs in southern Mongolia, where they found fossilized eggs of what they believed to be the early horned dinosaur *Protoceratops*. They thought the eggs belonged to *Protoceratops* because *Protoceratops* skeletons were the most common fossils found in the flaming red sandstone that forms the cliffs. In addition to the eggs and nests, they collected a whole series of *Protoceratops* skulls that document how the animal changed as it grew from a baby into adulthood.

Like everything in science, the conclusion that the eggs belonged to *Protoceratops* is subject to change based on new discoveries, and while the new dinosaur halls were being put together, such a discovery was made. Beginning in 1991, paleontologists and geologists from the American Museum of Natural History were invited by colleagues in the Mongolian Academy of Sciences to return to the fossil fields that Andrews and his crew had made famous. During the third year of this new expedition program, a fossil locality at which no one had ever collected before was discovered deep within the basins and ranges of the Gobi Desert. The name for the locality, like that of the Flaming Cliffs, was based on the surrounding topography. It was called Ukhaa Tolgod, which in Mongolian means "brown hills."

For a paleontologist, walking around outcrops of

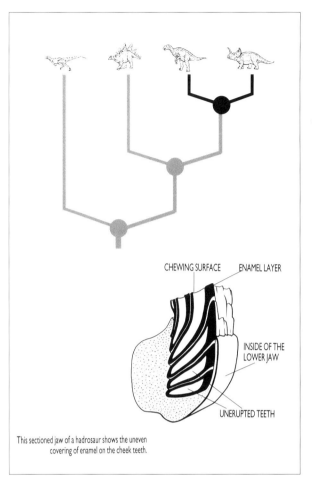

CHEWING SURFACE   ENAMEL LAYER

INSIDE OF THE
LOWER JAW

UNERUPTED TEETH

This sectioned jaw of a hadrosaur shows the uneven covering of enamel on the cheek teeth.

Cerapods have an uneven covering of enamel on their teeth. When the upper and lower teeth rubbed together as the animal chewed, the teeth wore unevenly and developed sharp ridges.

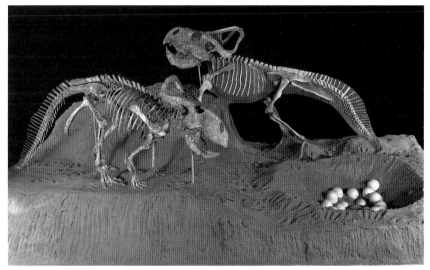

Protoceratops *was a primitive horned dinosaur from Mongolia that lived about 72 million years ago. The frill at the back of the skull is more well developed than horns.*

The Anatotitan *skeletons (left) and* Triceratops *(right) share the Hall of Ornithischian Dinosaurs.*

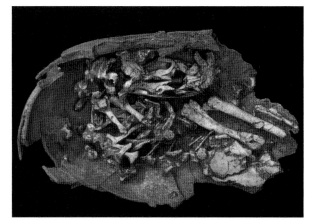

The 72-million-year-old embryo of an oviraptorid was found inside the kind of egg once thought to belong to Protoceratops.

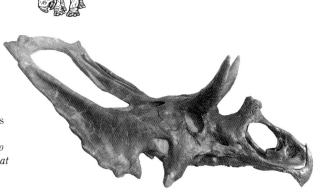

Chasmosaurus, *an advanced marginocephalian relative of* Triceratops *that lived about 75 million years ago, also had an extensive frill at the back of the skull.*

Pachycephalosaurus, *a 65-million-year-old marginocephalian, had a helmetlike dome of bone on the skull as much as six inches thick.*

sandstone at Ukhaa Tolgod was truly like being a kid in a candy store. The ground was littered with fossils of dinosaurs, primitive mammals, lizards, and nests with eggs. The shape of some of the eggs, as well as the surface texture of the shell itself, was identical to that of the eggs the Andrews expedition discovered at the Flaming Cliffs. At first, it was presumed that these, too, were nests and eggs of *Protoceratops.* However, fossils of *Protoceratops* were not very common at Ukhaa Tolgod. The most common dinosaur fossils at this new locality were those of a rare and unusual, toothless theropod called *Oviraptor.*

As prospecting for fossils continued, Mark Norell made an amazing discovery. Inside one of the eggs, the bones of an embryonic dinosaur were preserved. One glance was enough for his trained eye to discern that the expedition had just discovered the first embryo of a carnivorous dinosaur. After getting the specimen back to the museum, where the extremely delicate job of preparing the specimen could be done, it was discovered that the embryo, too, was that of an oviraptorid. As a result, several of the labels that we had written for the fossilized eggs in the exhibition had to be quickly modified to reflect our newly discovered knowledge, but that was a small price to pay for an enlightening piece of scientific progress.

Although the first dinosaurs eggs discovered did not turn out to be those of *Protoceratops,* the skeletons that the Andrews expedition brought back nonetheless provided the first clues about the early evolution of horned dinosaurs. Interestingly, most of the fossil skulls of this animal provide little evidence of horns, a feature that is prominently developed in the more advanced forms, such as *Triceratops, Centrosaurus, Chasmosaurus,* and *Styracosaurus.* However, *Protoceratops* does have the bony collar, or frill, that extends back from the rest of the skull over the neck region. The evolutionary beginnings of this feature can even be seen in the most primitive ceratopsian, *Psittacosaurus.*

It is the presence of this bony shelf at the back of the skull that provides the clue which relates horned dinosaurs to the bone-headed pachycephalosaurs. Members of both groups inherited this feature from a distant common ancestor, the first marginocephalian dinosaur, but the shelf evolved quite differently in the two subgroups. Instead of forming a bony collar that extends out behind the skull, the shelf in pachycephalosaurs forms part of the thick bony helmet that makes up the top of the skull. Not surprisingly, speculation abounds about the function of this helmetlike structure, which is as much as six inches thick in larger forms such as *Pachycephalosaurus.*

In 1955 Edwin H. Colbert proposed that the animals used them in demonstrations of head-butting to establish dominance, possibly in rituals revolving around feeding or mating. He observed that the skull and backbone are constructed in a way that might help absorb the impact of head-to-head collisions. More recently, other paleontologists have noted that such an impact on the rounded skull dome would tend to twist the neck, risking injury to the neck and spinal cord. Alternatively, some researchers have proposed that the skull caps were used to butt the sides or flanks of opponents, again as a means of establishing social dominance. But the reality is that we cannot test these ideas to be certain because we cannot observe the behavior of these extinct animals.

Arrayed in the alcove along the west wall of the hall are the duckbills and their early relatives, the euornithopods. Among members of this group, the jaw mechanism is constructed so that the joint between the upper and lower jaw lies below the level of the tooth rows. This arrangement, which evolved in the common ancestor, resulted in an extremely powerful, crushing action as the chewing musculature clamped the jaws together. With this lower position of the jaw joint, along with the raspy surface of the dental batteries, duckbills possessed an ability to grind up tough vegetation that was unmatched in other groups of dinosaurs.

One of the rarest specimens in our collection—the "mummy" of the duckbill *Edmontosaurus*—comes as close to answering the question of what an extinct dinosaur looked like as any fossil probably ever will. Most fossils are mineralized replicas of an animal's harder parts, such as bones or teeth. Only under the most unusual circumstances is any impression of the soft anatomy of an extinct dinosaur preserved. After death, the carcass must be quickly and deeply buried to prevent it from completely decaying or being scavenged. Then, the mud and sand that envelop the carcass must harden rapidly to form an internal or external impression of the skin before the muscles and flesh rot away. Our "mummy" has skin impressions preserved over several parts of the body that suggest a bumpy leathery texture similar to that on the foot of a chicken. This gives us a good idea of what the duckbill's skin would have been like to touch. Even more astounding is the webbing of skin that connected the three most prominent fingers on the hand. With just this one specimen, we can gain a pretty clear picture of what the form of this 65-million-year-old duckbill was like, but still we cannot determine the color of the skin. Today, more and more artists are depicting extinct dinosaurs in relatively bright colors and vivid patterns, but this simply represents the current fashion. There is no evidence to decide what color extinct dinosaurs were. The next time you draw a dinosaur, artistic license, along with the lack of any pertinent fossil evidence, gives you the right to make it any color or pattern you want.

The Hall of Ornithischians ends with an exploration of the possible reasons why these amazingly diverse groups of nonavian dinosaurs went extinct about 65 million years ago. It has been one of the most controversial topics in science during the 1980s and 1990s.

When it comes to dinosaur extinction, paleontologists have long tried to console their students and the public. More that 99 percent of all the species that have ever lived on the Earth are extinct, and the reign of the dinosaurs began over 228 million years ago. By contrast, the immediate evolutionary roots of humanity extend back only about four or five million years. Given that there are 18,000 kinds of birds living today it's not like dinosaurs got cheated. Nonetheless, duckbills and horned dinosaurs are not wandering around anymore. Why not?

There is now evidence to document two momentous global events at the time that nonavian dinosaurs went extinct: unusually voluminous volcanic activity and

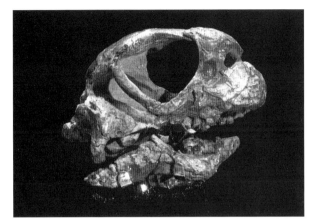

Psittacosaurus is the earliest-known horned dinosaur. It lived about 107 million years ago in Asia. This skull of a newborn is less than two inches long.

Below: The mummy of the duckbill dinosaur Edmontosaurus *preserves impressions of the skin, including webbing around some fingers of the hand.*

This impression shows the bumpy, leathery texture of the skin of Edmontosaurus, *which is like the skin on the lower legs and feet of a chicken.*

Here, the robotic skulls are sectioned in order to display the chewing abilities of these dinosaurs. The snout rotates away to reveal the tooth batteries in the upper and lower jaws.

A Look Inside the Jaws

pachycephalosaurs
and ceratopsians
MARGINOCEPHALIANS

These robotic dinosaurs contrast the chewing motions that characterized duckbills (left) and horned

catastrophic impact on the earth's surface of a large extraterrestrial object. Geologists have realized for decades that the end of the Cretaceous was marked by a large increase in volcanic activity. Huge volumes of lava erupted and spread over an extensive area of India; more explosive volcanism is recorded in deposits at the bottom of the South Atlantic Ocean near Antarctica; and numerous layers of volcanic ash representing eruptions associated with the uplift of the ancestral Rocky Mountains are preserved in ancient flood plain sediments now exposed in Wyoming and Montana. The largest event, which formed the thick sequence of basaltic fissure flows of lava in the Deccan Traps of India, began about 66 million years ago and ended just after 65 million years ago. All this volcanism would have spewed tremendous quantities of dust and sulfate aerosols into the atmosphere, causing reduced sunlight, acid rain, acidic layers of water near the surface of the oceans, a cooling of air temperatures, and depletion of the Earth's ozone layer.

The rising plumes of magma that fed these eruptions may have literally lifted the continents, causing the long-

What ended the age of the dinosaurs? One theory is that a large asteroid or comet impacted the earth near the present-day Yucatan Peninsula. Another is that there was an enormous volcanic eruption in what is now India.

recognized retreat of shallow seas back off the continents into the major ocean basins at the end of the Age of Dinosaurs. These seaways, such as the narrow one that extended from the Gulf of Mexico north to the Arctic across North America, had helped to maintain the equable, subtropical environments in which the dinosaurs thrived. Over a period of about 100,000 years, however, climates became more extreme as the seas retreated, with warmer days, cooler nights; hotter summers, colder winters. Conventional wisdom has long held that the cold-blooded dinosaurs could not tolerate these extremes and perished.

But why did the freezing winters and torrid summers not extinguish turtles, snakes, lizards, and crocodiles—cold-blooded animals that are at the mercy of the climate to maintain a livable body temperature? In addition, this was not the first time that the seas had retreated off the continents during the Age of Dinosaurs. Why did dinosaurs survive earlier marine regressions but not this one?

Such dissatisfaction with conventional gradualistic explanations led to a key observation that fostered the cata-

strophic scenario. In both marine and terrestrial rocks that span the end of the Age of Dinosaurs and the beginning of the Age of Mammals lies a thin bed of clay enriched in an element called iridium (Ir). Although rare in the Earth's crust because it sunk toward the core as the Earth cooled after its formation, Ir is enriched in many meteorites and comets, which preserve the original composition of material in our solar system.

Further examination of the boundary clay revealed the presence of microscopic crystals of quartz that were fractured in a pattern indicative of the intense temperatures and pressures generated by impacts. All this evidence led other scientists to propose that 65 million years ago, a large asteroid or comet collided with the Earth. It would have blasted an enormous dust cloud into orbit around the Earth which cut off sunlight for several months, inhibiting photosynthesis in plants; surface temperatures on land would then have dropped below freezing for several months; episodes of intense acid rain resulted; and eventually the surface temperature of the Earth would have risen as a result of the greenhouse effect. This disruption of the climate and food chain was proposed to have caused the extinction of dinosaurs within a period of several years.

In the early 1990s, a soberingly large crater was found buried deep beneath the layers of sedimentary rock that underlie the present coast of the Yucatan Peninsula in Mexico. Also, chaotically jumbled rock layers, which have been interpreted by many geologists to represent the damage created by "tidal waves," more accurately termed tsunamis, have been discovered in what is now Texas, Alabama, and Haiti. These areas formed the coastline around the Gulf of Mexico 65 million years ago. The jumbled rock layers are often associated with microscopic tektites, small droplets of glass generated by the enormous temperatures and pressures of the impact. Minerals from melted rock recovered from the crater, as well as tektites from Haiti, have been dated radiometrically at between 64.5 and 65.0 million years old, indicating the age of the impact.

Good geological evidence, therefore, supports both an impact and a large global episode of volcanic activity, but regardless of whether one favors a terrestrial or an extraterrestrial scenario, the question of how well we can "tell time" 65 million years ago directly affects our ability to test these ideas scientifically. Presently, our ability to estimate the period over which the large dinosaurs became extinct is limited by our techniques for determining the age of a rock through radiometric dating. Even the latest, laser-fusion equipment for $^{40}Ar/^{39}Ar$ dating yields ages with error factors of ± 10,000 to 100,000 years. These error factors do not allow us to distinguish the effects of an impact and its associated killing mechanisms, which were thought to have operated for only several years, from the possible longer term events associated with volcanic activity. Either event, or a combination of these and other factors, may have led to the extinction of nonavian dinosaurs. In reality, we just cannot be sure.

The extinction of the large dinosaurs has long been correlated with the beginning of what has been called The Age of Mammals, and the evolutionary roots of this group form the focus of the last two halls in the loop.

The 65-million-year-old Triceratops *had an impressive skull decorated with three horns and large frill.*

6 OUR ROOTS ARE AS OLD AS THE DINOSAURS

THE LILA ACHESON WALLACE WING OF
MAMMALS AND THEIR EXTINCT RELATIVES

THE LILA ACHESON WALLACE WING OF MAMMALS AND THEIR EXTINCT RELATIVES: THE MAJOR GROUPS AND THEIR EVOLUTIONARY RELATIONSHIPS

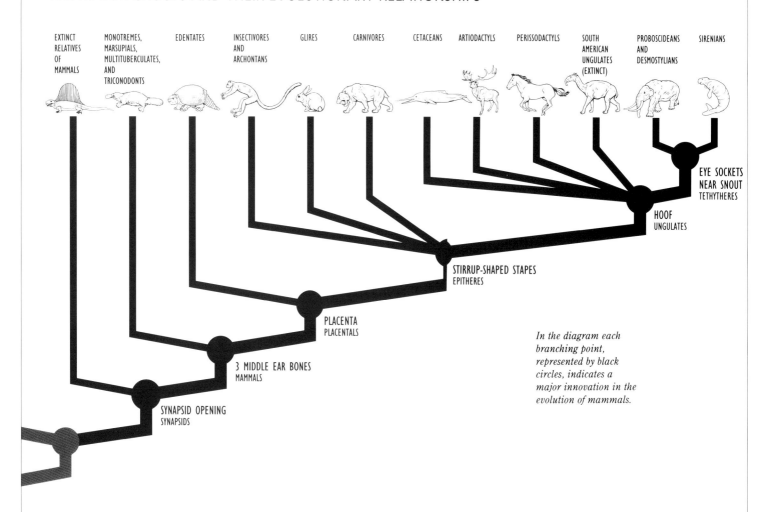

EXTINCT RELATIVES OF MAMMALS

MONOTREMES, MARSUPIALS, MULTITUBERCULATES, AND TRICONODONTS

EDENTATES

INSECTIVORES AND ARCHONTANS

GLIRES

CARNIVORES

CETACEANS

ARTIODACTYLS

PERISSODACTYLS

SOUTH AMERICAN UNGULATES (EXTINCT)

PROBOSCIDEANS AND DESMOSTYLIANS

SIRENIANS

EYE SOCKETS NEAR SNOUT
TETHYTHERES

HOOF
UNGULATES

STIRRUP-SHAPED STAPES
EPITHERES

PLACENTA
PLACENTALS

3 MIDDLE EAR BONES
MAMMALS

SYNAPSID OPENING
SYNAPSIDS

In the diagram each branching point, represented by black circles, indicates a major innovation in the evolution of mammals.

FOURTH FLOOR PLAN

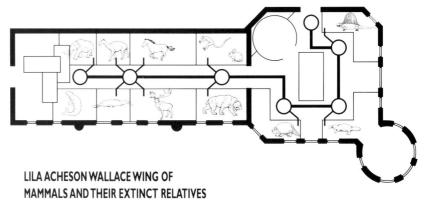

LILA ACHESON WALLACE WING OF MAMMALS AND THEIR EXTINCT RELATIVES
Evolutionary pathways are highlighted.

Having covered the branches on the evolutionary tree for dinosaurs, we now jump back down to the branching point where the mammalian lineage diverged from the reptilian one about 300 million years ago. In terms of evolutionary innovations, we are back at the point where the watertight egg evolved. This is the feature which probably allowed both mammals and their early relatives, as well as the reptiles, to colonize the land because they no longer had to return to the water to reproduce.

The fourth floor of the fifth building constructed within the museum has played host to a great variety of extinct animals since it was completed in 1896. The basic motif of columns and windows, designed by the architectural firm of Cady, Berg, and See, replicates those found in the Hall of Advanced Mammals. The windows within the Hall of Primitive Mammals provide a unique vista of Central Park and the skyscrapers along its southern border. Visitors are able to sit and rest in the circular tower that dominates the Museum's southeast corner (mirroring a tower at the southwest corner). Without doubt, these exhibits contain many of the world's ultimate evolutionary antiques, so we were encouraged to celebrate their significance in as classic a setting as we could provide.

First opened to the public in 1905 as the Hall of Fossil Reptiles, the exhibits in this hall included the enormous mount of *"Brontosaurus."* Subsequent to the original opening, *Allosaurus* and the *"Trachodons"* (now called *Anatotitan*) were added in 1907, and the upright *Tyrannosaurus* mount made its debut in this hall about 1915. In the 1920s and 1930s, the dinosaur specimens were moved into their new homes in the Halls of Early and Late Dinosaurs. It was not until 1957 and 1958 that planning and construction were initiated to develop this gallery into what was then called the Hall of the Giant Sloth. Eventually, the exhibition came to be known as the Hall of Early Mammals, which was developed under the guidance of George Gaylord Simpson and Malcolm McKenna. It opened to the public on 29 May 1965. In addition to the giant ground sloths, the presentation included skeletons of numerous, primitive, mammalian groups, as well as an orientation display about how fossils are collected and prepared.

The first animals encountered in the newly renovated Wing of Mammals and Their Extinct Relatives might be a bit surprising. A common character in many children's books about dinosaurs is *Dimetrodon,* a fin-backed animal that lived in North America about 280 million years ago. Although this animal used to be classified as a reptile, it is actually neither reptile nor a dinosaur. It lived about 50 million years before the earliest-known dinosaur, and in terms of its position on the evolutionary tree, *Dimetrodon* is much more closely related to you and me than it is to any reptile. The proof is found in its skull, where there is a small opening behind the eye socket. Muscles that closed the lower jaw probably attached around the edge of this opening. The same opening is found in all mammals, including you; it's the hole located between your eye socket and your cheekbone. The muscles that close your lower jaw run through this opening to attach on the side of your skull. We should take great pride in possessing this feature, because

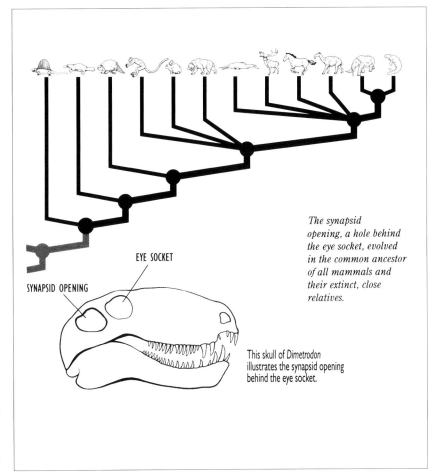

SYNAPSID OPENING   EYE SOCKET

The synapsid opening, a hole behind the eye socket, evolved in the common ancestor of all mammals and their extinct, close relatives.

This skull of *Dimetrodon* illustrates the synapsid opening behind the eye socket.

Dimetrodon,
an early relative of mammals, has a small synapsid opening behind its eye socket.

The WATERTIGHT EGG

sloths, armadillos, anteaters, and their relatives

EDENTATES

PLACENTA

AMNIOTES

TETRAPODS

GNATHOSTOMES

VERTEBRATES

Facing page: The entrance to the Hall of Primitive Mammals in the Lila Acheson Wallace Wing features the branching point for the watertight egg, a change that allowed both mammals and reptiles to reproduce on land.

This node explains the synapsid opening, a feature shared by all mammals and their extinct relatives. It is where muscles that close the lower jaw attach to the skull.

Tyrannosaurus *strides through the dinosaur hall in 1921. This hall also contained the mounted skeletons of* Apatosaurus *and* Allosaurus.

Below: *The present Hall of Primitive Mammals was once the dinosaur hall, shown here.*

Facing page: *Many dinosaurs, including the* Anatotitan *duckbill skeletons, were once crowded into the old dinosaur hall, shown here, that now contains the story of the early phases of mammal evolution.*

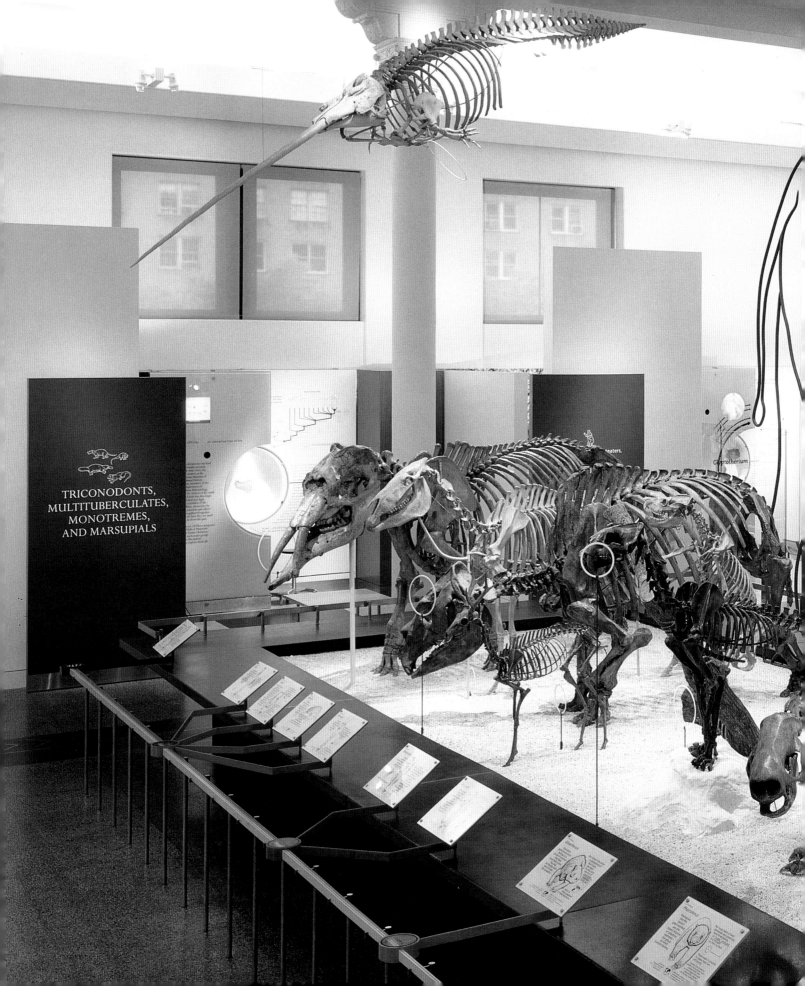

TRICONODONTS,
MULTITUBERCULATES,
MONOTREMES,
AND MARSUPIALS

An array of skeletons in the Hall of Primitive Mammals reveals the skeletal and ecological diversity of mammalian life, including the body outline and skull of the extinct Asian rhinoceros called Indricotherium.

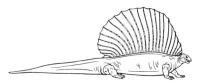

Edaphosaurus, *which lived in North America 280 million years ago, sported a fin supported by elongated vertebral spines.*

in terms of evolutionary relationships, this means that the lineage leading toward mammals, including us, extends as far back as that for reptiles.

Mammals and our extinct relatives have radiated into a dazzling diversity of forms that inhabit environments from the blistering sands of the Sahara to the frozen icepacks of the Arctic. An array of skeletons in the center of the first mammal hall, along with a video production in the adjacent theater, documents this diversity of adaptations—from flying bats to swimming narwhals, and from tiny shrews to 15-foot-tall rhinos.

The representative in this array for the earliest relatives of mammals, *Edaphosaurus,* documents that the evolutionary path leading toward our own group was not an easy one. *Edaphosaurus,* like *Dimetrodon,* sported a finlike structure on its back composed of elongated spines that extended up vertically from each vertebra over the ribcage. Although speculation abounds, no one can be certain just what, if any, function the fin served. Perhaps it helped regulate the animal's body temperature by warming the blood when the animal stood in the sun and cooling the blood when the animal stood in the shade. Or perhaps it served an important role in species recognition or mating rituals. Whatever the case, it is clear that there were at least some occasional disadvantages in lugging this thing around with you wherever you went. At some point during its life, one of the bony spines on the edaphosaur's fin was broken. If you look closely, you can see where the top part of the spine has been offset downward about an inch or two, so that it overlaps with the bottom part of the spine. During the healing process, the overlapping sections were fused together when the cells responsible for making bone deposited new material around the broken area. Because the healing process appears to have been carried to completion, we can be fairly certain that whatever caused the injury (and we really have no clues about this) did not directly result in the animal's death.

A little farther down the evolutionary path, we reach the branching point that represents the origin of our own group of vertebrates, mammals. Fossils of the earliest-known mammals are preserved in rocks almost 200 million years old, nearly as old as those containing the earliest-known dinosaurs. For the most part, these early representatives were rat- or shrew-sized animals. The oldest mammal in this exhibition, *Gobiconodon,* is only about 110 million years old and a bit larger than the earliest-known mammals. But how do we know these extinct animals that lived over 100 million years ago were truly mammals?

As most of us learned in our biology classes, mammals are vertebrates that nourish their young by producing milk from specialized mammary glands. In addition, almost all living mammals have a hairy covering on the body, and most give birth to live young. But these features are not preserved in fossils, so paleontologists need to use a bony feature for identifying mammals.

The feature most commonly used is found inside the ear. In reptiles and early relatives of mammals, like *Dimetrodon,* only one bone—the stapes—transmitted sound vibrations between the eardrum and the inner ear, allowing these animals to hear. Mammals, including you, have a more

128

specialized arrangement in which two additional bones—the incus and the malleus, help connect the eardrum with the inner ear. You may have been introduced to all three bones as the "hammer," "anvil," and "stirrup." The stapes is the stirrup-shaped bone in your ear. It was a more like a column in *Dimetrodon*. But where did the other two bones come from? Therein lies a most remarkable transformation, documenting how drastically bones can change their position and function during the course of evolution.

Paleontologists have collected a long sequence of fossils ranging in age from 300 million to 200 million years old. These early relatives of mammals, many of which are found in the first alcove of the hall, document the evolutionary stages leading up to the origin of mammals. Fossils of these animals show that the two additional bones in the ear of a mammal helped form the joint between the upper and lower jaws in early relatives of mammals. Over millions of years, these two bones became smaller and moved toward the back of the lower jaw, eventually becoming separated from it and joining the stapes to form a chain of three bones inside the middle ear. It may be that the three bones allowed mammals to hear across a wider or a more specialized range of frequencies, but it is difficult to be certain.

Following in the museum's long tradition of bringing these extinct mammals back to life for the public, we commissioned a series of illustrations to be done by one of the world's most gifted, contemporary, paleontological artists, Jay Matternes. In essence, we commissioned him to illustrate the more primitive representatives for several of the major groups of living mammals so that visitors could more easily understand where the evolutionary journeys for these groups had originated. Matternes's original illustrations are featured in a small gallery in this first hall of fossil mammals, and the most striking aspect of the drawings is their anatomical detail. This comes as no surprise to those of us who work with him because he is not only a gifted artist but also a meticulous anatomist. Matternes does not simply draw a fully fleshed-out extinct animal. Each animal is reconstructed through a series of three drawings. First, he makes a detailed illustration of the skeleton as he studies the fossil bones. Next, he restores the musculature on top of the skeleton using the closest living relative of the extinct animal as a guide. Finally, the last step is to layer on the hide over the musculature. Although there is certainly artistic license involved in the process, Matternes visually and verbally documents how each decision in the reconstruction is made, just as a scientist would document the steps in his experimental research. The result is essentially an artistic thesis based on the guidance provided by the curators in conjunction with his own insights. The finished illustrations must truly be seen to be believed.

At this point in the hall the limbs of the evolutionary tree for two of the three major groups of mammals branch off—monotremes and marsupials. Monotremes, including the platypus and the echidna, are the most primitive group of living mammals. Members of this group retain so many primitive features inherited from earlier common ancestors that monotremes are often called "living fossils." One example is their egg-laying mode of reproduction.

Until recently, the fossil record of monotremes presented

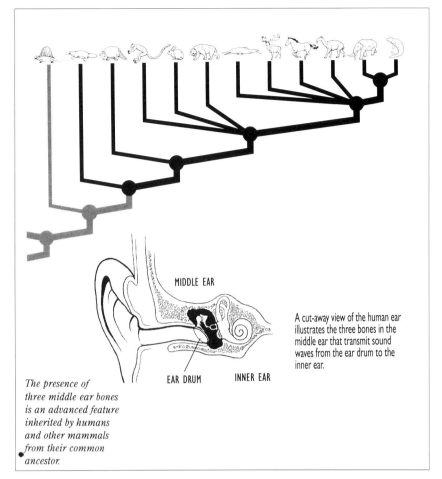

MIDDLE EAR

EAR DRUM   INNER EAR

A cut-away view of the human ear illustrates the three bones in the middle ear that transmit sound waves from the ear drum to the inner ear.

The presence of three middle ear bones is an advanced feature inherited by humans and other mammals from their common ancestor.

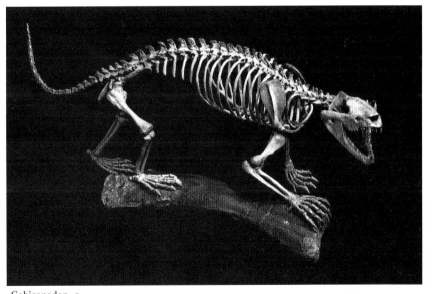

Gobiconodon, *a primitive mammal, lived about 110 million years ago in central Asia.*

The giant sloth, Lestodon, *shown in the Hall of Primitive Mammals, lived in South America 30,000 years ago.*

Below: Megaloceros, *the "Irish elk," lived until about 10,000 years ago. The largest deer ever, its huge antlers had an imposing 8-foot span.*

Facing page: Indricotherium, *a 30-million-year-old rhinoceros and the largest-known land mammal ever discovered, towers over the mammal diversity display.*

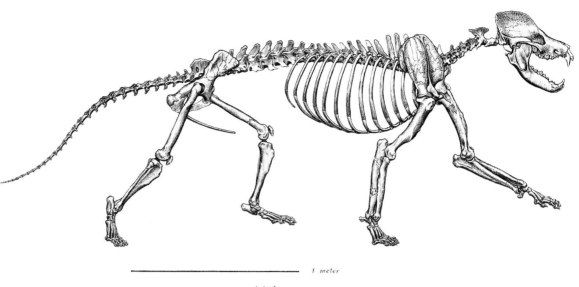

Paleontological artist Jay Matternes reconstructed the anatomy of a primitive bear-dog named Amphicyon *in three separate stages from the skeleton (top) to the fully fleshed-out animal (bottom).*

1 meter

1 foot

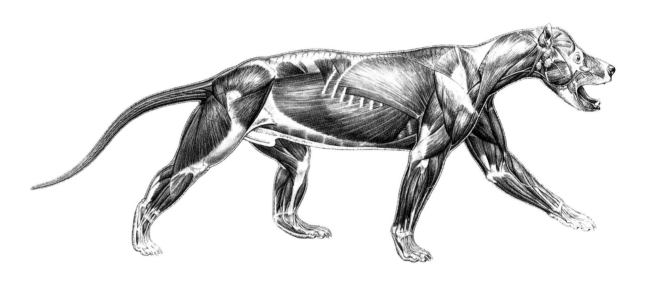

us with a serious contradiction. Although monotremes are relatively primitive in relation to other mammals, their fossil record extended back only about 25 million years. This perplexed paleontologists because marsupials and placentals as old as 100 million years had been discovered. But in 1982, the jaw of a small monotreme, named *Steropodon,* was discovered in the opal fields of Australia. This served to extend the fossil record for this primitive group also back to 100 million years.

Marsupials, like placentals, give birth to live young, but they are born at a much earlier stage of development and spend an extended period in the mother's pouch before they are ready to face the world on their own. Nonetheless, live birth is a feature that we have inherited from our common ancestor with kangaroos and koalas.

In general terms, we tend to think of marsupials as relatively small animals. But even as recently as 15,000 years ago at the end of the last Ice Age, a marsupial as large as a bison roamed the lake-dotted plains of Australia. This animal, called *Diprotodon,* is the largest marsupial ever known to have lived. About ten feet in length, it was probably the ecological analog of placental rhinos or hippos. But what was the largest land mammal ever known? You would never guess, even though I just mentioned the group to which it belongs.

Across from *Diprotodon,* on the island featuring the skeletal diversity of mammals and their extinct relatives, stands a striking metal sculpture of the body outline for the mammalian heavyweight champion. In fact, it was a rhinoceros, and this has been known for a long time. When we did the demolition in this hall to prepare for the renovation, we uncovered a painting of *Indricotherium* on one of the walls. In fact, the metal body outline was based on this painting, even though, as Malcolm McKenna pointed out to us, most paleontologists now believe that the animal was not as stocky as Osborn and his colleagues had originally shown it to be.

Indricotherium towered above its Asian contemporaries about 30 million years ago. Standing about fifteen feet at the shoulder, the animal was actually relatively slim and trim in relation to modern rhinos. It belonged to a group of running rhinos, noted for their relatively long, horselike legs, and although *Indricotherium*'s legs were not as slim as those of smaller models, they were still most impressively long. To provide a contrast between the size extremes into which mammals have evolved, the body outline of *Indricotherium* is juxtaposed against the skeleton of a contemporary, two-inch-long shrew.

From here, we move on along the evolutionary tree into other placental mammals, a group which was named for the advanced evolutionary feature which connects the growing embryo to its mother. More specifically, the placenta's soft tissues and blood vessels link the mother's bloodstream to that of the embryo. Through the placenta, the embryo receives nourishment and disposes of waste products. The placenta is also important in producing chemicals that control the time of birth for the embryo, which is born at a more advanced stage of development than in marsupials or monotremes.

The first group to branch off from the placental node

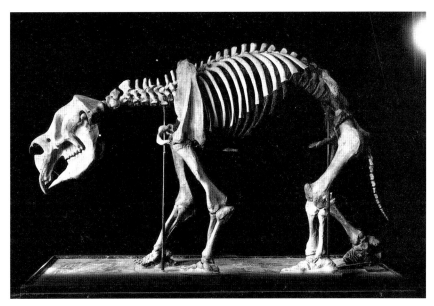

Diprotodon *is the largest marsupial ever known to have lived. It roamed Australia 20,000 years ago.*

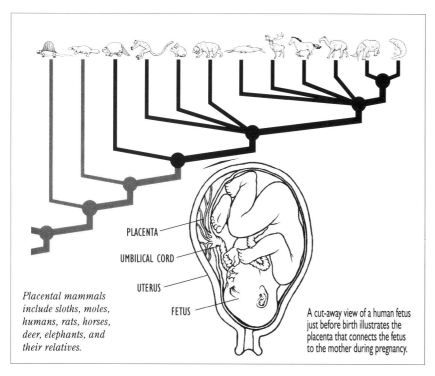

Placental mammals include sloths, moles, humans, rats, horses, deer, elephants, and their relatives.

PLACENTA
UMBILICAL CORD
UTERUS
FETUS

A cut-away view of a human fetus just before birth illustrates the placenta that connects the fetus to the mother during pregnancy.

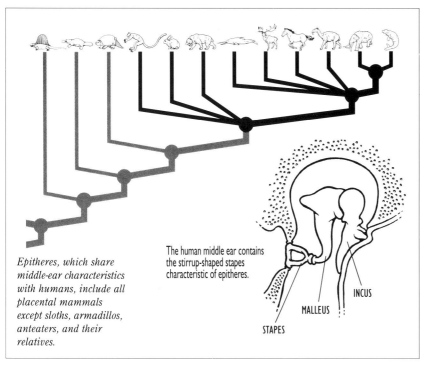

Epitheres, which share middle-ear characteristics with humans, include all placental mammals except sloths, armadillos, anteaters, and their relatives.

The human middle ear contains the stirrup-shaped stapes characteristic of epitheres.

INCUS
MALLEUS
STAPES

contains the edentates, such as sloths, anteaters, armadillos, and an extinct group called glyptodonts. These animals inherited a covering of bony armor from their common ancestor, and this armor was taken to an extreme in the armadillos and glyptodonts. In a sense, these are the mammals' evolutionary answer to the reptilian turtles and ankylosaurs. The entire length of the body is protected by bone. The structure of the armor covering, however, is different in the armadillos and glyptodonts. In armadillos, bands of bone stretch from side-to-side across the body. The bands are attached to one another by an elastic strip of skin so that, when threatened, the armadillo can roll up into a bony ball. In glyptodonts, the suit of armor is composed of hundreds of bony plates, which fit together like a mosaic to form a protective shield. Some had tails that ended in mace-like clubs, and even the skull of some glyptodonts was covered by a bony helmet.

One of my favorite specimens in the whole exhibit is a glyptodont skull. While I was doing some reading in preparation for helping to write the exhibit script for this alcove, I came across a passage in a scientific journal that referred to a glyptodont specimen that appeared to have died from a bite through the top of the skull. To my surprise, the author of the article listed the catalogue number of the specimen as a fossil in our museum's collection. At the time I thought to myself, that might be an interesting story to tell in the exhibit if the specimen is not out on loan being studied. I went down to the collection floor where the specimen would be housed and began looking through the drawers. Sure enough, there it was.

Two oval puncture wounds were present on top of the skull just behind the snout. As the principal curator of the mammal halls, Richard Tedford, interpreted it, a large predator had seized the juvenile from the front, either to knock it over or immobilize it so that other predators could attack it. Although we do not know the identity of the attacker, the most likely candidate is a jaguar-sized cat. Bones of such cats have been found in deposits laid down at the same time as those in which the glyptodont was found. The bite appears to have been lethal because there is no evidence of the bone around the wounds having healed.

Moving into the second hall of fossil mammals, The Paul and Irma Milstein Hall of Advanced Mammals, we are confronted with a complex evolutionary puzzle. Despite a great deal of research involving not only comparative anatomy but also molecular biology and genetics, the order in which the major groups of placental mammals branched off the trunk of the evolutionary tree is not very clear. This is illustrated by the fact that several major branches of the tree are tied to this branching point, including carnivores, rodents, rabbits, insectivores, bats, and even the group of mammals to which we belong, the primates. All these groups, including the hoofed mammals encountered along the trunk of the tree farther down the hall, evolved from a common ancestor in which the original ear bone, the stapes, is shaped like a stirrup. We do not know what advantage, if any, this shape conveys to the group, but in many of these animals, a major blood vessel that serves the brain runs through the hole in the stirrup.

One reason why the evolutionary sequence remains

Facing page (middle): Panochthus, *a 30,000-year-old glyptodont, was armored like a traveling tank and is related to living armadillos.*

Above: *In the glyptodont display a* Panochthus *stands behind the skull of a juvenile glyptodont that has two puncture wounds in the top of the skull thought to have been inflicted by a large carnivore.*

unclear may be that there appears to have been a very rapid rate of evolution among mammals at the close of the Age of Dinosaurs and the beginning of the Age of Mammals between 70 million and 60 million years ago. Perhaps the later phases of this evolutionary burst had something to do with the extinction of nonavian dinosaurs about 65 million years ago, which would have left many ecological niches for large carnivores and herbivores available for other animals to exploit. These are difficult problems to test so long after the fact. In short, this difficulty of reconstructing the sequence of evolutionary events illustrates a common problem in evolutionary history: the available anatomical and genetic evidence gleaned from living relatives and the fossil record does not always point to a clear sequence. As a result, several groups of placental mammals are shown branching from this point on the evolutionary path.

In fact, Henry Fairfield Osborn developed this hall from the start as a showplace for his own true paleontological love, fossil mammals. The hall is contained within the third building constructed in the museum complex. It was designed by the firm of Cady, Berg, and See, and was completed in 1894. The Hall of Fossil Mammals opened to the public in November 1895. Although the mammoths and mastodons were moved into this hall in the late 1960s, when Section 2 was transformed into the Hall of Earth History, no major renovation of the space had been attempted since Osborn first opened his Hall of Fossil Mammals a century ago.

Just through the entrance into the newly renovated Hall of Advanced Mammals lies our own home in the exhibition. In a sense, we just barely made the cut. We share this alcove with rodents, rabbits, insectivores, and our closest non-primate relatives, the bats. Surprised about our next of kin? So was I when I first heard about the idea.

Primates and bats are both members of a larger group of mammals called archontans. We all arose from a common ancestor that had ankles built to allow a lot of flexibility. Most of our primate relatives live in trees, as do most of the other archontans. A flexible ankle appears to have played a role in roosting and climbing.

Whereas bats evolved the ability to fly with their arms, primates developed the ability to grasp objects with both their hands and feet. The highly opposable thumb, much more opposable than that of saurischian dinosaurs, for example, is the key to our grasping capability because the thumb can be rotated into a position in which it can be pressed up against the tips of the other fingers. A moment's reflection establishes how important this grasping ability is for important human activities, such as feeding and writing. We can thank our common ancestor with other primates for providing us with the basic anatomical structure to make these activities possible.

Our exact position in the hall is represented by the cast of a skullcap of *Homo erectus,* located near the northeast corner of the room. We did not want to use a lot of space to discuss human evolution in these halls because the museum had recently opened an entire, magnificent, diorama-filled hall devoted entirely to human evolution and human biology.

I should point out, however, that, with the backing of our

Top: The American Museum of Natural History consisted of three buildings in 1894; it now fills twenty-three buildings.

Bottom: Primates, along with bats, are members of a group called archontans. In the Paul and Irma Milstein Hall of Advanced Mammals, a small, early primate called Notharctus *(right) that lived 49 million years ago shares an alcove with* Homo Erectus *and* Palaeocastor, *all animals that arose from an ancestor with highly flexible ankles.*

The Hall of Fossil Mammals first opened to the public in 1895, on the fourth floor of the Museum's third building, where the Paul and Irma Milstein Hall of Advanced Mammals is now located.

whales, dolphins,
and their relatives

CETACEANS

The magnificent new Paul and Irma Milstein Hall of Advanced Mammals is dominated in this view by the skeleton of the "Irish elk," Megaloceros (left); the Warren mastodon, Mammut (middle);

One of the oddest
animal homes is this
spiral-shaped burrow,
the "Devil's corkscrew."
It was once thought to
be the remains of
ancient tree roots.

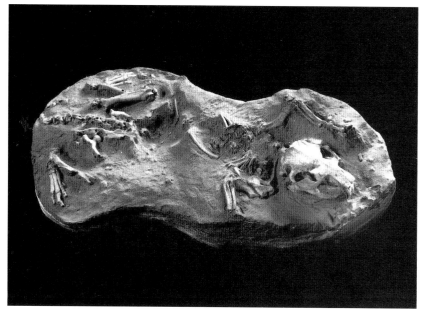

Palaeocastor, *an*
ancient beaver that
lived 23 million years
ago, built these
impressive burrows
for homes.

paleoanthropological advisor Eric Delson, we intentionally placed the primate branch of the mammalian tree in the middle of the mammal halls. In the eighteenth century, scientists wrestling with the biological concept of evolution placed humans and other primates at the top of a ladder of life that they pictured as a "Great Chain of Being." The implication was that humans represented a higher, more advanced form of life than other organisms. We now have a vastly different evolutionary perspective. Rather than resembling a ladder, evolution is more like a tree with many branches, none of them being higher or better in an evolutionary sense than any other. In fact, the last or highest branch in our halls, as we shall soon see, is reserved for the noble elephants and seacows. I doubt that more than a few contemporary humans would vote for those groups as representing the pinnacle of mammalian evolution. Yet they deserve the title as much as any other group. Who would deny that they are not as unique or as well-suited to their natural environment as we are?

As mentioned earlier, insectivores include the smallest living mammals. The adult of one species of shrew weighs less than a dime, and its entire body is only about 2.5 inches long. These animals are primarily burrowers, and they inherited a prominent depression on the side of the snout where the strong muscles that move the nose and lips attach to the skull.

Far and away the most diverse and abundant group of mammals are the rodents. Although the degree of kinship is still a matter of active debate, one piece of anatomical evidence that suggests rodents and rabbits are closely related is the presence of an enlarged pair of central incisors at the front of the upper and lower jaws. In both groups, these are used for gnawing and cropping the vegetation that they eat.

Rodents constitute more than 40 percent of all living mammalian species. To give you some sense of this diversity, just listen to a few of the different kinds of animals that belong to this group: mice, rats, lemmings, gophers, porcupines, kangaroo rats, tree squirrels, flying squirrels, chipmunks, chinchillas, capybaras, guinea pigs, groundhogs, and even beavers. Environmentally, rodents are also diverse, living in habitats that range from the tundra to the jungle to the desert.

To me the most unique element of the rodent display is not a rodent itself, but rather the former home of a rodent. Most of us are familiar with the modern beaver's uncanny engineering skills, which are put to use constructing elaborate wooden dams across streams and building wooden lodges within the resulting ponds. In the past, however, beavers fashioned different kinds of lodgings. We now know that North America was once home to a group of terrestrial, burrowing beavers, and the burrows they built long puzzled the early residents of the Great Plains.

In the last decades of the 1800s, fossil collectors prospecting in western Nebraska often came across large, spiral-shaped structures, commonly termed "Devil's corkscrews," in the banks of badland gullies. Their unusual form catalyzed a lot of speculation about what they represented and how they were formed. Ideas ranged from fossilized plant roots to the fused remnants of lightning strikes.

Not until 1906 was the mystery solved, when paleontologists found the 23- million-year-old skeleton of an extinct beaver at the bottom of one of the corkscrews. Closer inspection occasionally reveals tooth and claw markings on the sides of these corkscrews, suggesting that the beavers dug the burrows with their incisors and cleared away the loose dirt with their feet. A small chamber off the main burrow, several feet above the bottom, appears to have served as a combination living room and bedroom, and its position helped to guard against the living chamber becoming flooded.

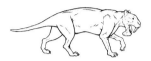

Moving across the hall, the name for the alcove containing the largest group of meat-eating mammals, Carnivora, is somewhat misleading. Almost all the members of this group are, in fact, carnivorous, but there are mammals that do not belong to this group that also eat meat. For example, in Australia and South America, many extinct marsupials appear to have filled the niches for large carnivores that placentals do on continents of the northern hemisphere. One example is the saber-toothed marsupial *Thylacosmilus,* which terrorized the denizens of South America about four million years ago. Even among placentals, many whales fill the roles of large carnivores in marine environments, but they do not belong to the group Carnivora.

What makes some carnivores card-carrying members of the Carnivora? The answer is found in the dentition. Carnivorans, including cats, hyenas, dogs, bears, seals, raccoons, weasels, and their extinct relatives, all inherited from their common ancestor a specialized pair of teeth for slicing meat. These teeth, called the carnassials, consist of the last premolar in the upper jaw and the first molar in the lower jaw. In many carnivorans, such as the true saber-toothed cat *Smilodon,* these teeth become greatly enlarged, although, in the case of *Smilodon,* not as large as the canine teeth that form the sabers.

The fossil skeleton of *Smilodon* in our exhibition is a bit unusual in at least two ways. First, most of the saber-toothed cat skeletons that one sees in North American museums come from the La Brea Tar Pits in Los Angeles. Our skeleton, however, represents the South American species, *Smilodon necator,* which lived about 25,000 years ago in Argentina at the end of the last Ice Age. As we saw in the museum's *Tyrannosaurus* specimen, it is clear that life was not always blissful even for an intimidating carnivore. Although the right side of the skull of *Smilodon necator* is studded with a magnificent six-inch-long saber, only a nub of the canine is present on the left side. What happened? Upon closer examination, you can see that at some point in the animal's life, the end of the saber broke off, perhaps as it was trying to wrestle down large prey. Although the sabers are impressively long, they are also relatively thin from side to side. As a result, if the prey twisted violently while the sabers were imbedded in the gut or another part of the body, they could easily break. What is more, the nub of our *Smilodon*'s saber is not jagged, but worn down to a smooth rounded surface. This documents that the animal survived the injury and lived into late adulthood despite the handicap, although it must have suffered through a few painful meals after the injury first occurred.

The next branching point explores the evolution of a more commonly recognized anatomical feature, the hoof.

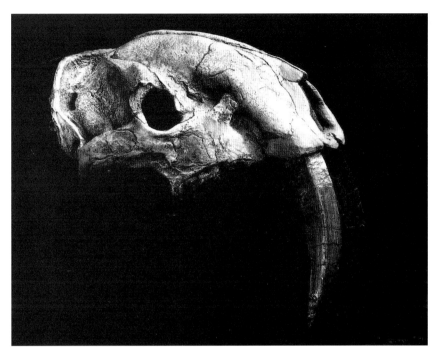

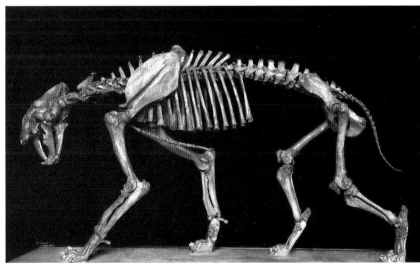

Top: Thylacosmilus, *while similar to a placental saber-toothed cat, was actually a marsupial with saberlike canine teeth that lived in South America 4 million years ago.*

Bottom: *Brandishing a six-inch-long saber tooth, the 25,000-year-old placental saber-toothed cat,* Smilodon, *snarls menacingly.*

141

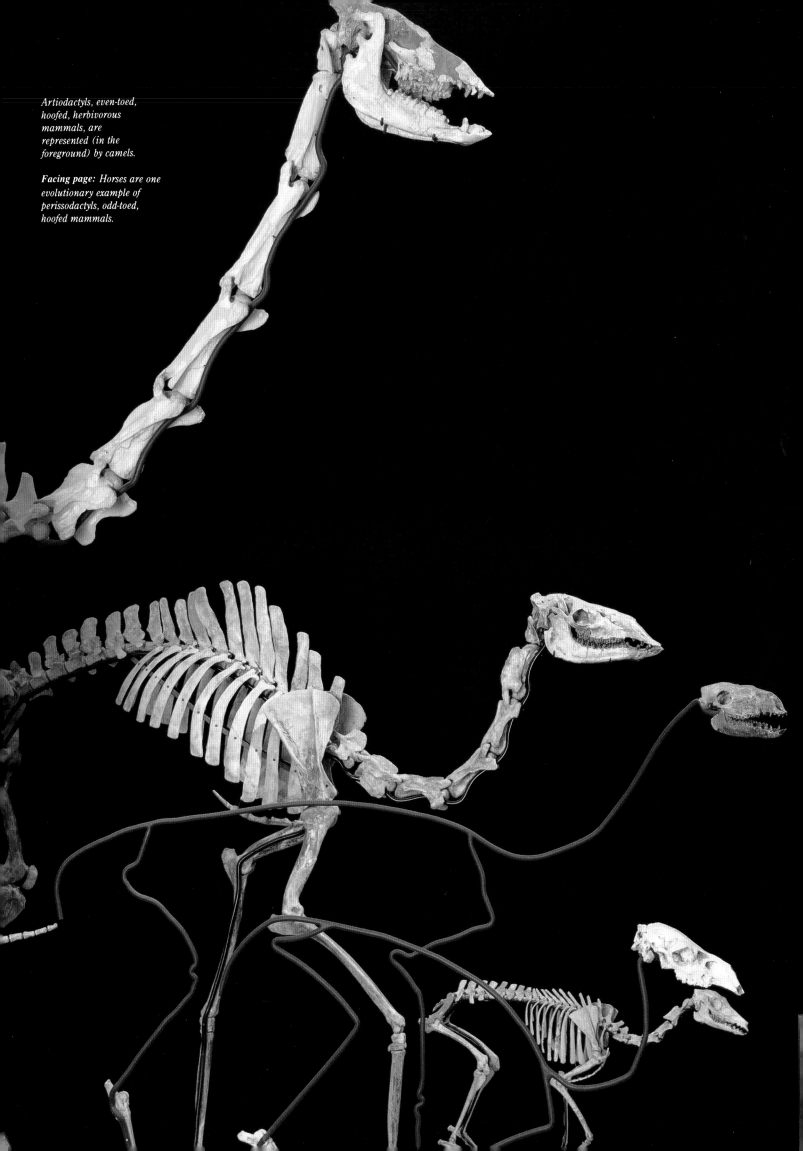

Artiodactyls, even-toed, hoofed, herbivorous mammals, are represented (in the foreground) by camels.

Facing page: *Horses are one evolutionary example of perissodactyls, odd-toed, hoofed mammals.*

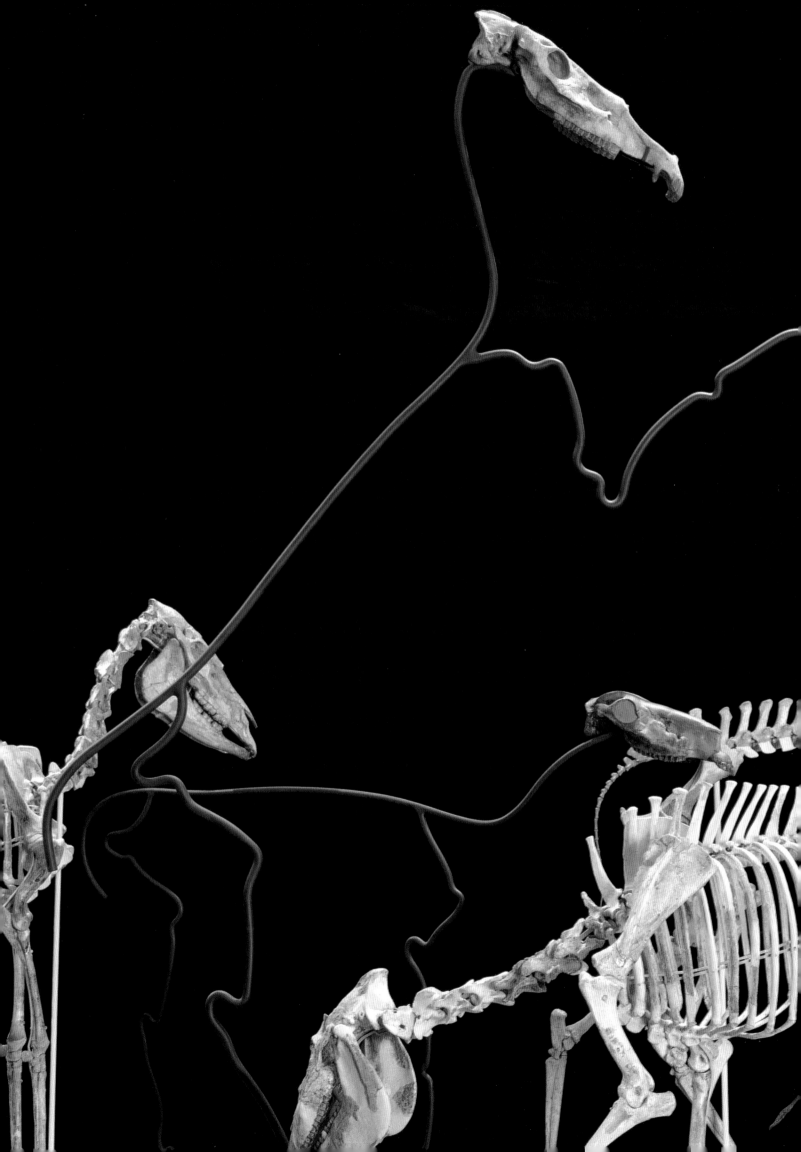

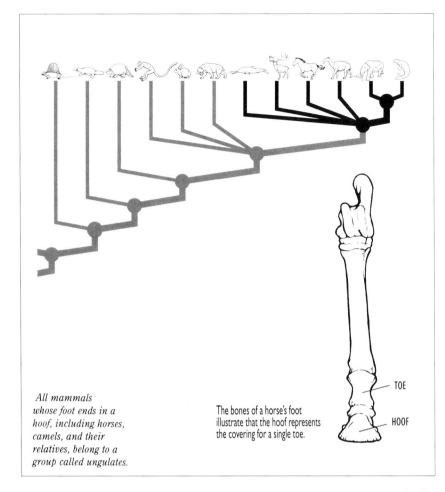

All mammals whose foot ends in a hoof, including horses, camels, and their relatives, belong to a group called ungulates.

The bones of a horse's foot illustrate that the hoof represents the covering for a single toe.

TOE

HOOF

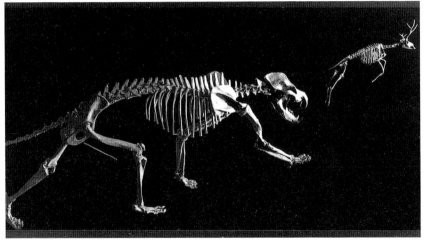

Amphicyon *lunges after antelopelike* Ramoceros, *which leaps for survival in this 14.5-million-year-old chase scene.*

Hooves evolved from claws simply by broadening the surface of the last toe bone that touches the ground. In many hoofed mammals—or ungulates—the number of toes on each foot has been reduced from five to only one or two, so the hoof alone must provide traction and a stable foundation when the animal walks or runs. Examples of ungulates include pigs, camels, deer, horses, rhinos, whales, elephants, seacows, and their relatives.

Along the main path between the alcove for carnivorans and the one for even-toed hoofed mammals, an unusually dramatic and dynamic mount was created by Phil Fraley's mounting crew. This 14.5-million-year-old chase scene features a distant relative of bears and dogs, *Amphicyon,* closing in on an antelopelike contemporary, *Ramoceros.* The scene is set on the mud flat of a freshwater lake that once dotted the landscape of what is now California's Mojave Desert. As *Amphicyon* prepares to make its final lunge, *Ramoceros* launches itself into the air in one last desperate leap for survival. Who won? Who knows?

The nine-foot-long, pacing stride of *Amphicyon* is clearly documented in the fossilized trackway below the skeleton that the animal left on the ancient mud flat. The springy yet spindly legs of *Ramoceros* provided this animal with a formidable ability of evasive agility. The mount thus symbolizes the age-long interaction between mammalian predators and prey. The fastest, most efficient hunters are the ones most likely to sustain themselves through capturing the prey that allows them to survive and reproduce. Similarly, the most agile and elusive prey are the ones most likely to avoid capture and pass on their inherited features to the next generation. And so the story continues even today.

Ramoceros is a representative of the group of ungulates that possesses an even number of toes on their feet, the artiodactyls. Other commonly recognized members include pigs, peccaries, hippos, camels, deer, antelope, sheep, goats, oxen, cattle, and bison. All these animals arose from a common ancestor with an ankle bone that had pulley-shaped surfaces on both the top and bottom of the bone. The ridges of the pulley on the top fit into grooves in the bottom of the shin bone, while the ridges of the pulley on the bottom help form the ankle's joint with the rest of the foot. This structure serves to provide a very stable joint between the foot and the rest of the leg; in other words, the foot cannot rotate from side-to-side, but only in a fore-aft plane.

Even before domestication by humans, artiodactyls spread around the globe, especially throughout the northern hemisphere, but for me, the roots of one group appear to have begun in a place that I would never have guessed. That group is the camels, which include not only the single-humped dromedary of the Arabian regions and the double-humped Bactrian form of Asia, but also llamas and their South American kin. None of these present-day, geographic distributions prepared me for the fact that the oldest-known camel fossils come from North America. Animals like the four-toed *Poebrotherium* roamed the plains of the midwest about 36 million years ago. Even as recently as ten or eleven thousand years ago, at the end of the most recent Ice Age, camels were wandering around what is now Beverly Hills. The fossils from the Tar Pits prove it.

Across the hall is the alcove for the other main group of ungulates, the perissodactyls. This group, which includes tapirs, rhinos, horses, and a couple of extinct groups, arose from a common ancestor with an odd number of toes on the feet, in which the middle toe was the longest and most well developed. It was from looking within the lineage leading to the modern horse that American paleontologists were able to formulate one of the earliest strong cases to support the existence of evolutionary change through time.

As soon as he had founded the Department of Vertebrate Paleontology at the museum in 1891, Henry Fairfield Osborn began sending field parties to join in the "bone rush" for fossils in the western half of the United States. The exploits of some of the most famous collectors and expedition leaders, such as Barnum Brown and Roy Chapman Andrews, have already been mentioned in connection with the Halls of Saurischian and Ornithischian Dinosaurs. But the first field trips to the West were not intended to collect dinosaurs. Rather Osborn sent his staff to search for fossil mammals beginning with an expedition to the Big Horn Basin of Wyoming in 1891, and over the next few decades, one of the people most responsible for managing this quest for mammalian fossils was a gangly, young paleontologist named William Diller Matthew. Under his field direction an immense collection of fossil horses began to flood into the museum, and under Osborn's supervision, Matthew compiled the first comprehensive exhibition on the evolution of the horse.

Many of the trends within horse evolution were first presented to the public as part of this exhibit, trends that are still recognized by students of horse evolution today: a general increase in size, an increase in the length of the cheek teeth, and a reduction in the number of toes on the foot. These trends were so visually compelling that by placing the skeletons of *"Eohippus," Orohippus, Mesohippus, Merychippus, "Pliohippus," "Plesippus,"* and *Equus* in a line around the southwest corner of the hall, it appeared that evolution had orchestrated an undeviating, 55-million-year-long march that culminated in the modern horse. This straight-line approach to evolution suited Osborn's social values, which were closely, although in retrospect rather perversely, tied to the progress of our own species.

Both Osborn and Matthew, however, knew from the fossils that were being collected that the real pattern of horse evolution was much more complex. The evolutionary tree for horses that accompanied the exhibit documented, for example, that some of the later horse genera, such as *Archaeohippus,* were actually smaller than their earlier relatives. In fact, 15 million years before the advent of the modern horse, evolution produced a form of comparable body size in *Hypohippus.*

Matthew was acutely aware of these facts because he kept impeccable field notes about where in the sequence of rocks different kinds of horse fossils were found. These, along with his own ideas about how horse evolution had proceeded, led him to construct the most comprehensive picture of horse evolution available at the time. In essence, our revised display of horse relationships simply represents an extension of Matthew and Osborn's original presentation. In front, the stately evolutionary progression from

"*Eohippus*" (now called *Hyracotherium*) to *Equus* is visually summarized. However, in the back row, the bushy diversity that characterized Matthew's collections, along with numerous subsequent discoveries, provides a clearer view of the group's evolutionary complexities. Dynamic metal sculptures for several of these fossil genera were fabricated to provide visitors with a clearer image of these extinct animals' body size. For those in the audience who are not satisfied with simply seeing, real fossils of the teeth in some of these horse genera are literally brought within reach of the visitor. And one of the genera that occupies an important step toward the evolution of the modern horse is represented by a particularly poignant pair of individuals inside the perissodactyl alcove.

Protohippus was a three-toed horse that populated the Great Plains around present-day Nebraska, and on one day about 12 million years ago, a tragic event appears to have occurred. At first glance, the fossil plaque reveals the exquisitely preserved skeleton of an average-sized adult. But an additional, partially hidden set of tiny bones is seen to occupy a position just behind the rib cage and underneath the pelvis. Upon closer inspection, you can make out a small skull and well-formed eye socket, the slender lower jaw, and the elongated bones of one of the front feet. One likely explanation for this association of skeletons is that a mare may have died while trying to give birth to her foal. In this case, the problem appears

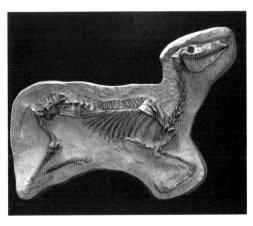

to be that of a breech birth, in which the hind feet, rather than the forefeet and head, emerged first. The foal was apparently not able to fully emerge from the mother's birth canal, which not only caused its death but may have led to an infection that caused the mare's death. If true, this scenario would constitute an ancient illustration of a still common problem for horses and other ungulates. Within a few hours after being born, the young must be able to walk and keep up with the herd, and the long, well-formed limbs required for locomotion become an unwieldy part of the birthing process.

Right past the alcove for perissodactyls, the exhibition contains a small area for several groups of unusual South American ungulates. For most of the Age of Mammals, between about 65 million years ago and 3 million years ago when the Isthmus of Panama formed, South America was an island continent. During this period, a unique set of placental mammals evolved to fill the niches occupied by other placental groups in North America, Europe, and Asia. Examples include the rabbitlike *Propachyrucos,* the rhinolike *Toxodon,* the horselike *Thoatherium,* and the camel-like *Macrauchenia.* Once the Panamanian Isthmus formed, many North American placentals, including several carnivores, invaded the formerly isolated habitats of these South American ungulates. By the end of the last Ice Age about 11,000 years ago, all these indigenous ungulates were extinct.

Fossils sometimes capture a moment, like this 12-million-year-old Protohippus *mare and its unborn foal preserved under the hips.*

Desmostylians such as the 20-million-year-old Palaeoparadoxia (left) were relatives of seacows (right) and elephants.

Facing page:
The hoof was an important evolutionary development inherited from the common ancestor of all ungulates, or hoofed mammals.

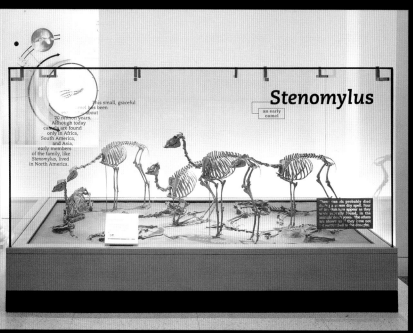

This small, graceful ... camel has been ... about 20 million years. Although today camels are found only in Africa, South America, and Asia, early members of the family, like Stenomylus, lived in North America.

Stenomylus

an early camel

These ... can ... probably died ... g a ... were dry spell. Four of ... such ... appear as they were actually found, in the animals' death poses. The others are shown as if they have not ... subscribed to the drought.

The skeletal depiction of an ancient bedding ground for a primitive camel called Stenomylus illustrates both the living and death poses of this 20-million-year-old animal.

Mammals whose foot has a

HOOF

belong to a group called ungulates.

The hoof evolved when the bone at the end of one or more toes broadened and became overlaid with a thick,

horny covering
made of material
like your nails.

Ungulates include pigs, camels, deer, horses,
rhinos, whales, elephants, sea cows, and their relatives.
Clearly, some of these animals, such as whales,
no longer have hooves,
but evidence shows that the mammals
from which they evolved did.
Consequently, they belong to the ungulate family.

What is the hoof for?

Located at the end of the foot, they obviously play
a major role in locomotion.
In many ungulates, such as horses and deer,
the number of toes on each foot has been reduced to only one or 2.
Their strength and mass provide traction
and a stable base to give the animal when it walks or runs.

pigs, deer, cattle,
and their relatives

ARTIODACTYLS

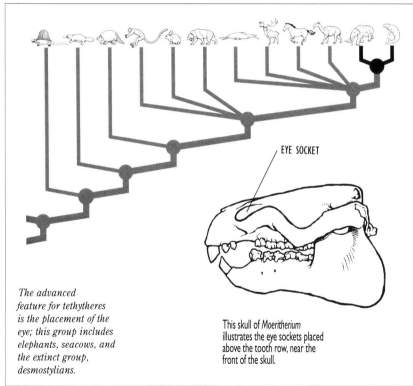

The advanced
feature for tethytheres
is the placement of the
eye; this group includes
elephants, seacows, and
the extinct group,
desmostylians.

EYE SOCKET

This skull of Moeritherium
illustrates the eye sockets placed
above the tooth row, near the
front of the skull.

Of all the evolutionary journeys undertaken by mammals over their 200-million-year history, the most remarkable is probably that of the whales. The reason is simple. Whales did not start out in the water; instead, they reverted to living in an aquatic environment just like their earliest-known vertebrate relatives.

The immediate evolutionary roots of whales can be traced back over 50 million years to large, carnivorous land mammals, such as *Andrewsarchus* from Asia and *Harpagolestes* from North America. The tall narrow cheek teeth of these animals are very similar to those found in the earliest true whales such as *Pakicetus*.

Most of the evolutionary changes found in whales are related to their aquatic lifestyle. The common ancestor of whales passed along modified front limbs to all later whales. Instead of using the front legs for walking or running, whales have flippers with extra bones in the fingers that are covered by a webbing of skin. The flippers help to steer and stabilize the animal as the powerful tail, with its strong, fleshy, horizontal flukes, propels the body through the water. Because whales have lungs rather than gills, they must return to the surface to breathe; some modern whales, however, have developed the ability to hold their breath and stay underwater for more than an hour. When they do return to the surface, the air is expelled from the lungs through the nostrils, which are located not at the end of the snout but high up on the skull between the eye sockets. This process of exhaling generates the geyserlike spouting behavior that has become such a popular attraction for sightseers.

Many kinds of whales retain conical teeth for eating fish and other animals. Examples include killer whales, sperm whales, and dolphins. It seems ironic, however, that the largest whales, such as the blue whales, are not only toothless, but also eat some of the smallest organisms in the ocean. In place of teeth, blue whales and their relatives possess fringelike curtains, formed by shredded material similar to that in your fingernails, which hang from the jaws. In effect, this substance, called baleen, acts like a net to filter out the small plankton as the whale swims through the water with its mouth open.

After viewing the largest mammals that have ever lived, the visitor moves into the last part of the hall, which is dominated by a group that contains the largest living terrestrial mammals. The group is called tethytheres, and it contains elephants, seacows, and their extinct relatives. The name comes from the Tethys, an ancient ocean around whose shores the earliest representatives of the group are generally found. It included the present-day Mediterranean Sea, extending from Gibraltar on the west, across the Middle East, and connecting with the Indian Ocean to the east. These animals inherited from their common ancestor a skull on which the eye sockets are placed toward the front above the teeth. It is not clear what, if any, adaptive value this feature affords.

Among tethytheres, elephants and their extinct relatives are most closely related to an extinct group called desmostylians; both groups have the ear opening located high on the skull. Desmostylians were stocky, four-legged animals that appear to have lived along the coast of the

North Pacific. Their body proportions resembled those of hippos. Because fossil remains of these animals have been found exclusively in marine sediments, most paleontologists agree that desmostylians were at least partially aquatic, but the degree to which they pursued an aquatic lifestyle is a matter of some debate.

Elephants, mammoths, mastodons, and their close relatives belong to a group called proboscideans. The name refers to the trunk, which was well developed in all the later members of the group. This versatile appendage represents a fusion between the muscles, skin, and other tissues in the upper lip and the nose. The trunk is used for breathing, feeding, drinking, vocalizing, and even fighting. The feature that later proboscideans inherited from the common ancestor was tusks. Even the earlier proboscideans, such as the 35-million-year-old *Moeritherium* from Egypt, had a pair of slightly enlarged incisors in the upper and lower jaws. Later proboscideans took the enlargement of these tusks to an extreme, such as in the shovel-shaped lower tusks of *Platybelodon* and the magnificent, gracefully curved upper tusks of the mammoth.

Standing on one side of the giant mammoth skeleton is the skeleton of the Warren Mastodon—one of the more famous specimens in our collection. Discovered in 1845 near Newburgh, New York, this skeleton became the focal point of a museum in Boston built by the anatomist John C. Warren. Just after the turn of the century, in 1906, the acquisitive Henry Fairfield Osborn arranged for the purchase of the specimen with the help of J. P. Morgan. In the next year, after a renovation of the skeleton and a reconstruction of the mount, the Warren Mastodon made its New York debut to broad public acclaim.

Resting on the other side in the shadow of the huge mammoth skeleton is the relatively minute mummy of a baby woolly mammoth, complete with face, trunk, and left front leg. Its leathery hide represents the freeze-dried remains of the animal's original skin. It was found in 1948 during the process of hydraulic mining for gold. The carcass was recovered in three sections, which were subsequently stitched together in a rather Frankensteinian collage after the remains were embalmed. This small animal inhabited the area around present-day Fairbanks, Alaska, about 21,000 years ago. The mysteriously forlorn look on the animal's face becomes even more poignant when we recognize that the carcass provides no evidence of what caused the baby's death.

The last branch on the evolutionary tree of mammals is occupied by seacows and their relatives. The dense bone of their skeletons, in which the marrow cavities are either very narrow or nonexistent, provides a kind of ballast to help keep them submerged when they feed on sea grasses or seaweed.

When visitors reach the end of the evolutionary tree in the exhibition, we want to provide them with a sobering reminder. They will have just experienced 500 million years of vertebrate evolution, but drastic changes in a continent's fauna can take place over much shorter periods. Take our own continent, for example. The Knight murals from the old Ice Age Hall, which now dominate the northern wall of this last mammal hall, illustrate that just 10,000 years ago, at

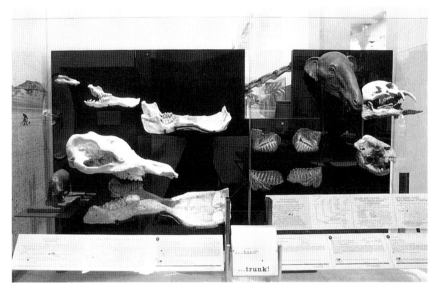

Top: Elephants and their relatives belong to a group called proboscideans. They share a flexible trunk and enlarged incisors—which we recognize in living elephants as tusks.

Bottom: *Effie is the nickname given to this 21,000-year-old mummy of a baby woolly mammoth. The parts present include a head with trunk and the left front leg.*

*These paintings by the
famed nature painter
Charles R. Knight depict
scenes from the
Pleistocene Period.
Originally mounted in
the Hall of the Age of
Man, they now grace
the Paul and Irma
Milstein Hall of*

CHAS. R. KNIGHT
1916

Top: A paleontologist hunts for fossil treasure near the Flaming Cliffs of Mongolia during an American Museum of Natural History expedition in the early 1990s.

Bottom: In the laboratory, a preparator removes matrix from the vertebrae of Tyrannosaurus.

Facing page:
The curving tusks of the gigantic, 11,000-year-old mammoth greet visitors.

the end of the last Ice Age, the fauna of North America was much different. Many of our visitors have driven across the country to visit this exhibition. Just imagine what they would have seen if they had crossed the continent just 500 generations earlier in their family's history. Giant ground sloths, armored glyptodonts, mammoths, mastodons, saber-toothed cats, and even camels would have been roaming the plains and valleys. Now they are all gone. Many scientists believe that overhunting by early human populations played at least a partial role in this episode of extinction. Whether or not our species played such a role in that event, we are certainly agents of extinction in today's world. Over the short life of this exhibition during the next several generations, what effect will we have on the diversity of vertebrate life that evolution has taken 500 million years to produce?

In the renovated mammal halls, a computer interactive display allows people to explore how fossils are discovered and collected. Once a paleontologist is in the field, he or she walks over the hillsides and ravines looking for scraps or fragments of bones that might be littered on the surface. This process, called prospecting, has all the excitement of a treasure hunt.

When a fragment is found, the paleontologist carefully picks and brushes away the rock around the fossil in order to determine how much of the animal is there. As the fossil is exposed, he squirts glue into cracks that run through it to keep it from breaking apart. Then he digs a trench around the specimen before covering it with wet tissue. The tissue serves to separate the fossil from a layer of plaster-soaked burlap that is applied next. After it hardens, the plaster and burlap form a cast to protect the fossil, just like doctors put a cast around a broken arm or leg. Then the cast is dug completely out of the ground.

But that is just the start of a fossil's journey. Once the cast is dug up, it is carefully labeled so that the contents and the place it was collected will be easy to identify when it arrives back at the museum. It is then packed in a crate to be shipped. Once at the museum, the crates are unpacked and the casts are checked for damage. They are cut open with a saw, and the long, delicate process of preparation begins.

Fossil preparators, like those on Jeanne Kelly's crew, are exceptionally skilled artisans. Often working with the specimen under a microscope, they use dental tools, miniature sand blasters, grinders, and brushes to clean away the rock that still surrounds the fossil. Sometimes the grains of sand must be picked away from the fossil bone grain by grain. In addition to having extensive technical and anatomical knowledge, a preparator requires an infinite amount of patience and dedication. Just one fragile specimen can take weeks or even months to prepare, especially if a lot of natural cracks and fractures run through the specimen. In such cases, broken pieces must be glued back together as they are cleaned. For larger specimens, this is done in a sand box. The sand helps stabilize the bone in the desired position as the glue dries. Once the bone is glued and the preparation is complete, the specimen is ready for study by the curators or other scientists. The preparators went through this process dozens of times to make new specimens ready for this exhibition.

PERISSODACTYLS

horses, rhino
and their rela

TETHYTHERE

Eye sockets near the snout
evolved in the common ancestor of

HOOF

EPITHER

you
are here

7 WHAT'S THE POINT?

Through the ribs of an 11,000-year-old mastodon we look back down the main path in the Paul and Irma

Real fossils, like this mammoth, present anatomical evidence for evolution, while allowing the visitor to see the striking beauty and majesty of vertebrate life.

The renovation of The Halls of Vertebrate Evolution has been a very time-consuming and expensive undertaking. Few other natural history museums would have been in a position to even consider a project of this scope because of space limitations and financial considerations. Yet, for this institution, and especially for those of us who have worked on the project, it assumed the spirit of a scientific crusade. It is interesting to reflect back on why we became so motivated.

Our mission as an institution is to inform the public about the natural world. In order to catch people's interest, we must present scientific information in an entertaining way because museums now must compete with other activities and attractions for the public's leisure time. In fact, there is a prominent, contemporary school of exhibition design that advocates giving the visitor only what he or she asks for as a way to ensure that the exhibition is popular.

I vehemently disagree with this philosophy. At this institution, we have an extremely diverse audience. We cannot pitch all the information to the lowest common denominator of interest and intellect. It is true that about 500,000 school children per year come through the museum, and we must stimulate their curiosity to learn by providing them with easily understandable elements in the exhibition. These children, however, grow up to become adults, and our surveys tell us that among our adult visitors, 59 percent are college graduates, and 31 percent have attended graduate school. We have a responsibility to challenge, as well as to entertain this sophisticated audience. We fail in our mission if we provide visitors only with what they think they want when they walk through the entrance. It is not enough for them to walk out with smiles on their faces. Clearly, that reaction is better than a frown, but we succeed in our mission only if visitors walk out of the museum feeling that their intellectual horizons have broadened.

Furthermore, our responsibility to help educate the public is tied into a growing social problem that is beginning to receive a lot of attention. There is currently profound concern about the "scientific literacy" of the public, both in the United States and throughout the world. Nowhere is the literacy of the public more suspect than when it comes to evolution. This is, at least in part, because of all the loaded philosophical issues that evolution raises. Nonetheless, we thought we could make a contribution to the public's understanding of science in general and their own evolutionary heritage in particular by using the popular vehicle provided by dinosaurs and other fossil vertebrates.

One of the most important goals of this project was to present a summary of the anatomical evidence for evolution. Cladistically based treatment of relationships, tied to the evolutionary tree motif, provided a direct way in which to illustrate this body of evidence. But the goal was not simply to present information about evolution; the power of the exhibition derives from the display of real fossils. It is the genuine anatomical evidence for evolution, and you cannot get that anywhere else. Moreover, this approach allowed us to emphasize that humans are an integrated part of this evolutionary pageant, not an entity that is isolated from it.

There is also great concern in scientific and public circles about the rate at which species are going extinct on this planet as a result of our environmental and technological expansion. We humans tend to view our world from only a present-day perspective and to place all our focus on the briefest snapshot of the 4.5-billion-year-long movie that comprises the history of our planet. The exhibition should help visitors understand that it has taken evolution 500 million years to produce the diversity of living vertebrates that we see today. The Timelines computer system, which uses a chronological approach as the primary organizing framework, will be most helpful in clarifying this immense expanse of time. Since our whole presentation utilizes a cladistic approach, the exhibition will be very helpful in illustrating the anatomical changes that occurred to produce that diversity. It is important for the public to comprehend both perspectives if they are to be informed partners in the process of addressing the issues raised by today's "biodiversity crisis," because it is through the cladistic approach that scientists evaluate the diversity of life.

By laying out the exhibition based on evolutionary relationships, we are also highlighting one of the major areas of on-going research at this museum. The public tends to think of the museum as a place to view exhibits; however, few people realize that our scientific staff actively contributes information to this body of evolutionary knowledge.

Even more important, however, is that the public gains a better understanding of how scientific ideas are proposed and debated. Although we may want to know everything about extinct organisms, there are limits to the kinds of questions we can ask of the fossil record. As scientists, we must ask only questions that we can test with the available evidence. Unfortunately, there is no direct evidence to test many of the speculations proposed about how extinct vertebrates behaved. We, as paleontologists, need to be more forthcoming about this limitation when we present our ideas to the public. We need to explain the hypotheses as well as the evidence used to evaluate the hypotheses and be honest about the strength of the conclusions made. Otherwise, we leave a false impression about both how science works and how much we really know.

It is because of this problem that much of the public distrusts scientists and scientific research. Because we often sound so certain and authoritative about our conclusions, many of which do not hold up under the scrutiny of further testing, the public has come to see science as a search for the truth rather than as a comparison of different points of view designed to glean the most reasonable explanation from the available body of evidence. We have set ourselves up to be viewed as incompetent when our tentative conclusions are overturned as the result of normal, healthy scientific re-evaluation and testing. Consequently, exhibits that illustrate the process of debate and that engage visitors in reaching their own conclusions about controversial topics are the ones that will most aid in promoting scientific literacy and developing a better awareness of how science can help illuminate our world.

The opportunity to learn more about the history of our planet and its life forms has been the greatest reward of working on this renovation, not only for myself but for all of the talented people who have participated. We in turn, hope that visitors of all ages who are interested enough to come to see the exhibition halls will leave with new knowledge about their extended family ties to life on Earth.

INDEX

Note: Page numbers in *italics* refer to illustrations.

ILLUSTRATION CREDITS

Except where noted, all illustrations © copyright American Museum of Natural History. Numbers refer to page numbers.

American Museum of Natural History guidebooks to Hall of Vertebrate Origins, Halls of Dinosaurs, Hall of Mammals and Their Extinct Relatives: cladogram and node cladogram diagrams (adapted from original designs by Ralph Appelbaum Associates): 44, 45, 48, 53, 56, 57, 64, 68, 69, 76, 82, 84, 92, 96, 100, 101, 109, 120, 121, 129, 134, 144, 148.

Ralph Appelbaum Associates: overall cladogram and graphic design of floor plans: 12, 32, 36–37, 44, 68, 100, 120.

Rob Barber: paintings, 34–35, 38–39.

Jackie Beckett: 18–19, 23, 27, 40, 42–43, 46, 62–63, 69, 76, 78–79, 83, 86 top, 87 top, 93 top left, 96, 97, 101, 107, 108 bottom, 117, 142, 143, 144, 153.

Jackie Beckett/Denis Finnin/Craig Chesek: 2–3.

Craig Chesek: 54 bottom left, 55 top left, 58 top left and bottom left, 129 bottom, 140 bottom.

Lowell Dingus: 152 top.

Mick Ellison: 112 top.

Denis Finnin: 22, 26, 50 top and bottom , 51 top and bottom, 54 (top left, top right, bottom right), 55 (bottom left, top right, bottom right), 58 (top right, bottom right), 59, 64, 93 bottom, 94 top, 113 top, 116, 123, 130 top and bottom, 135, 136 bottom, 140, 141 top, 145, 146 top, 148, 149 top and bottom, 156.

Denis Finnin/Ben Blackwell/Craig Chesek: cover, 1, 81, 86 bottom, 87 bottom, 94 bottom, 95 top and bottom.

© Scott Frances/Esto: 10–11, 14–15, 66–67, 71, 74–75, 90–91, 98–99, 102–103, 106, 110–111, 114–115, 118–119, 122, 126–127, 131, 138–139, 146 bottom, 147, 154–155.

© John Gurche: painting, 29.

Ed Heck: reconstruction drawings: 12, 36–37, 44, 48–61, 64, 65, 68, 69, 76, 81, 82, 84, 92, 93, 96, 100, 101, 108, 109, 112, 113, 120, 121, 128, 129, 133, 134, 135, 140, 141, 144–146, 148, 149.

Frank Ippolito: anatomical illustrations within cladogram diagrams: 45, 48, 53, 56, 57, 64, 69, 76, 82, 84, 92, 96, 101, 109, 121, 129, 134, 144, 148.

Charles R. Knight: paintings, 24, 150–151.

© Jay Matternes: drawings, 132.

© 1996 Louis Psihoyos/Matrix: 25 top and bottom.

Jeff Speed: 30–31.

Dennis Wilson: 82 bottom, 88 top and bottom, 113 bottom, 140 top, 152 bottom.

ARCHIVAL PHOTOGRAPHS

Courtesy Department of Library Sciences, American Museum of Natural History

Pages: 8 top, negative #471; 8 bottom, neg. #474; 9 top, neg. #368; 9 bottom, neg. #313169; 16, neg. #35383; 20, neg. #69183; 21, neg. #314524; 32, neg. #313086; 33 top, neg. #37797; 33 bottom, neg. #39131; 47 top, neg. #337978; 47 bottom, neg. #32918; 49, neg. #322199; 57, neg. #317590; 60, neg. #35041; 61, neg. #46509; 65, neg. #39129; 70, neg. #322530; 72 top, neg. #315930; 72 bottom, neg. #326179; 73, neg. #600800; 77 bottom, neg. #2A21932; 77, neg. #38715; 80, neg. #2A2690; 82 middle, neg. #2A2786; 84 bottom, neg. #35422; 85, neg. #33605; 89, neg. #311977; 92 bottom, neg. #310100; 93 top left, neg. #2A21966; 93 top right, neg. #319836; 93 bottom, neg. #2A21972; 104, neg. #311978; 105, neg. #327562; 108, neg. #310269; 109, neg. #314857; 112 top, neg. #602317; 112 middle, neg. #314114; 112 bottom, neg. #319456; 113 top, neg. #602315; 113 middle, neg. #330491; 121, neg. #315862; 124 top, neg. #38713; 124 bottom, neg. #38714; 125, neg. #34797; 128, neg. #35338; 131, neg. #310314; 134 middle, neg. #35948; 136, neg. #476; 137, neg. #499; 141 bottom, neg. #5433.